WISE UP AND LIVE! is a book of wisdom from Proverbs that meets us where we are and begins to move us to where God wants us to be.

WISE UP AND LIVE! has down-to-earth applications of Christian discipleship as it is to be lived, taught and felt. These selections from Proverbs cover relationships with: God, self and others.

WISE UP AND LIVE! emphasizes that Proverbs is one of the most comprehensive statements of divine wisdom in all literature. These capsules of wisdom are more than clever hints about how to run your life. They convey a deep spiritual insight that points to the Person of all wisdom, Jesus Christ. Knowing Him rather than memorizing a list of rules and catchy phrases, is the secret of "wising up and living!"

WISDOM FROM PROVERBS

WISEUP
& LIVE!

G/L
REGAL
BOOKS ™

A Division
of G/L
Publications
Glendale,
California,
U.S.A.

PAUL E. LARSEN

Other good reading in the Bible
Commentary for Laymen series:
Patterns for Power—Parables of Luke
   D. Stuart Briscoe
Highlights of the Bible—Genesis – Nehemiah
   Ray C. Stedman
Pass It On—1 & 2 Timothy
   Robert H. Mounce

The foreign language publishing of all Regal books is under the direction of GLINT. GLINT provides financial and technical help for the adaptation, translation and publishing of books in more than 85 languages for millions of people worldwide.

For more information write: GLINT, 110 W. Broadway, Glendale, CA 91204.

The *Authorized King James Version (KJV)* is the basic Bible version used in this book. Other Bible versions used are:
New American Standard Bible. © The Lockman Foundation 1960, 1962, 1963, 1968, 1971. Used by permission.
The Living Bible, Copyright © 1971 by Tyndale House Publishers, Wheaton, Illinois. Used by permission.

Seventh Printing, 1980

Published by
Regal Books Division, G/L Publications
Glendale, California 91209
Printed in U.S.A.

Library of Congress Catalog Card No. 73-86222
ISBN 0-8307-0453-1

CONTENTS

FOREWORD

Paul Larsen was once my pastor. For some months, during his Pasadena days, I sat under his preaching with as much regularity as my own schedule allowed. In few periods of my life have I been more stimulated, enlightened, encouraged, and admonished from the pulpit.

In *Wise Up and Live!* you can get a taste of Paul Larsen's thinking and preaching. I am glad you can for many reasons. First, it deals with an area of the Scripture which most preachers bypass with disciplined regularity. Every year a group of my students tackle projects on the book of Proverbs. Every year I send one or two of them to riffle through the library and discover sermons based on these brief, terse, pungent Old Testament sayings. Year by year they come up virtually wanting. At last I have a book I can put in their hands to show them what can happen when a man of God works his way into the world of Proverbs.

Second, this book is well-lighted with illustrations. Like windows, they let the light in so that the basic point the Scripture is making will be bright and clear to our eyes and hearts. Larsen has constructed a solarium, a hothouse of windows through which the light of God's truth can pass to warm and nurture our spiritual growth.

Third, in these pages we find a great many of the major themes of Scripture examined, applied and celebrated. Paul Larsen has more than a feel for Christian theology. He has a great appreciation of what God is doing in creation, in history, and in the person of Jesus Christ. He is able to see the connections between the various themes. This theological perspective keeps him from preaching on the Proverbs moralistically, from reducing them to legalistic regulations or philosophical advice. He sees what God is doing and saying through the whole Scripture, and he lets those deeds and words furnish the context for Proverbs.

Fourth, the words of Israel's wise men contribute remarkably to our understanding of the perils, foibles, and possibilities of human experience. It is no accident that when the greater-than-Solomon came, the Wise Man whom wise men worshiped, much of what He said and taught was based on the message and style of His predecessors in Proverbs. Paul Larsen will help us understand them and Him.

Finally, the down-to-earth applications of these chapters will prove helpful. We deal not with vapid theory, not with idle speculation, not with vague generalizations, but with Christian discipleship as it is to be lived, taught, felt. Here is reading not only for the study but for the kitchen, the living room, the bedroom, the shop, the store, the office. Only a pastor whose heart has been open to the needs of hundreds of his people can write like this.

This is a book that meets us where we are and begins to move us to where God wants us to be. *Wise Up and Live!* needs no commendation from me. It will make its own way with power and clarity. I eagerly share it with you in order that a man who has been my pastor and my friend may enrich your life and ministry as he has mine.

Dr. David Allan Hubbard

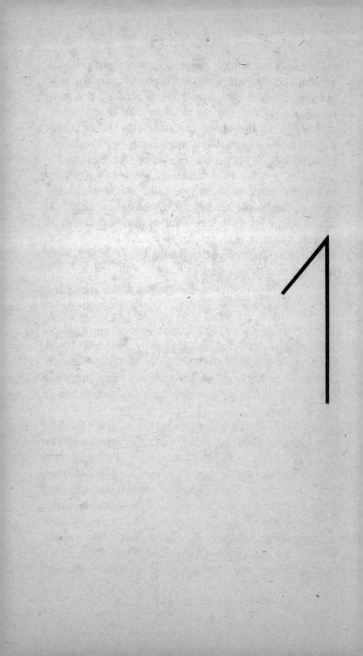

THE
PURSUIT
OF
WISDOM

The Bible contains many types of literature. There is history, as in the books which tell the story of Israel, or Acts, which tells the history of the early church. There are collections of sermons, as in the prophets. There are books of doctrine and instruction, as in the epistles.

But there is a body of literature in the Old Testament which is known as "wisdom" literature. The wisdom literature in the Bible includes Proverbs, Job, Ecclesiastes and the Song of Solomon. Sometimes, for convenience, we include the Psalms, though they technically are not the same kind of wisdom literature.

The books of Proverbs has at least three different authors. King Solomon is the main writer; two others, Agur and Lemuel, are also named (Prov. 30:1; 31:1). Newly discovered archeological evidence demonstrates that during the very time that Solomon lived, a thousand years before Christ, there was throughout the entire Middle East a vast body of wisdom literature. In fact, Agur and Lemuel were probably not even Israelites, but kings of neighboring nations.

God has always been concerned about all people, not just the Jew. In Proverbs, the use of material from non-Israelite sources shows that God has witnesses beyond His chosen people.

As a matter of fact, there are many parallels between these biblical Proverbs and proverbs found in other Near-Eastern literature. This does not mean that the Hebrews borrowed it lock, stock and barrel, but that it was part of a literature which, under divine inspiration, finds its place in our Bible.

It is interesting to note the literary form of the Proverbs. Many of the statements are phrased as couplets, or two-line sayings that are complete in themselves. There are several types of couplets. One is the antithesis, where the second phrase is a contrast to the first phrase: "A cheerful heart does good like medicine, but a broken spirit makes one sick" (Prov. 17:22, *TLB*).

Another is the comparison, where the second phrase strengthens the first phrase: "A rebuke to a man of common sense is more effective than a hundred lashes on the back of a rebel" (Prov. 17:10, *TLB*).

A third type uses imagery, such as the simile, to illustrate the point: "He sticks to his bed like a door to its hinges" (Prov. 26:14, *TLB*).

Some Proverbs come in the form of prayers: "O God, I beg two favors from you before I die: First, help me never to tell a lie. Second, give me neither

Prov. 25:1
Prov. 22:17
2 Peter 1:20 + 21
Prov. 6:16-19 octastich

poverty nor riches! Give me just enough to satisfy my needs! For if I grow rich, I may become content without God. And if I am too poor, I may steal, and thus insult God's holy name" (Prov. 30:7-9, *TLB*). Interesting philosophy! Give me just what I need.

What is the essence of the wisdom of which the wisdom literature speaks? Wisdom is distinct from knowledge in the general sense. It is not simply the capacity to grasp great bodies of learning—to know about the solar system, to know about microbiology and bacteriology, to know about the laws of physics. It is not the mere amassment of knowledge. If mere knowledge is the same thing as wisdom, there are many "wise" men who are really fools. This, by the way, is where we get the word sophomore. That's a Greek word for "a wise fool." By the time you're in tenth grade you know a little bit; but the trouble is you think you know everything. That makes a fool of you.

I like the description in Proverbs 1:2: "He [Solomon] wrote them to teach his people how to live—how to act in every circumstance. . . ." (*TLB*). Wisdom is *truth for living*—it teaches you how to come to grips with the realities of the universe so that your life will be meaningful and successful.

Truth for living: this has been one of the great foundations of the structure of Hebrew thought. Hebrew thought had little interest in what the Greeks called "philosophy," the ultimate principles that stand behind things. Important as those may have been, the Israelites just said, "I want to know what I need to do as a person to get on in life." That was the Jewish mood.

Wisdom is seeing things from God's point of view.

Truth for living is not abstract truth. It means you have to do something; not just to know something but to do something. Look at a few examples: "An empty stable stays clean—but there is no income from an empty stable" (Prov. 14:4, *TLB*); "Reverence for God gives a man deep strength; his children have a place of refuge and security" (Prov. 14:26, *TLB*); "Anyone who oppresses the poor is insulting God who made them. To help the poor is to honor God" (Prov. 14:31, *TLB*).

This is wisdom that has to do with how to live. It recognizes that to *know* the right is not necessarily to *do* the right. When a man knows the right and does the right he is a wise man. It is the wedding of knowing and doing—it is the junction of the good and the true.

The book of Proverbs goes deeper even than just giving truth for living. While the Proverbs are a very useful thing to put into our minds to guide us, simply memorizing them will not in itself give a man a wise and happy life. If we reduce wisdom simply to short little sayings we shall soon be confused about how to apply them.

Many of the Proverbs even seem to contradict each other. You're supposed to be good to the poor and the stranger, as we just saw, but the same book of Proverbs tells us you're a fool if you're surety for a stranger! (See Prov. 6:1; 11:15.) How do you join these two together without having a contradiction? The only thing we can say is that sometimes you ought not to be surety for a stranger, and other times you ought to be generous.

But something begins to happen in Proverbs which

points to the fact that wisdom is more than clever little sayings, little hints about how to run your life. Wisdom, in the Proverbs, becomes a person. Wisdom is personified.

We do the same thing today. We personify Mother Nature, for example. We say, "Mother Nature made it this way." "Mother Nature made it that way." "Mother Nature is bringing out the flowers." Have you ever met her? Except among the animists, does anybody worship her? We have taken one of the great elements of life and personified it—made it into a person.

The personification of wisdom takes place in the first nine chapters of the book of Proverbs. These chapters contain not the traditional little sayings found in the rest of the book, but rather a document by Solomon in which he speaks of wisdom as though it were a person.

Notice this: "Wisdom shouts in the streets for a hearing. She calls out to the crowds along Main Street, and to the judges in their courts, and to everyone in all the land: 'You simpletons!' she cries. 'How long will you go on being fools? How long will you scoff at wisdom and fight the facts? Come here and listen to me! I'll pour out the spirit of wisdom upon you, and make you wise'" (Prov. 1:20–23, *TLB*).

Now if you'll come to the New Testament you'll see some very interesting things. Jesus Himself uses the personification and carries it along when He says, "Wisdom is vindicated by her deeds" (Matt. 11:19, *NASB*). Paul takes the personification of wisdom another step—indeed, the final and most profound

Matt. 11:19
1 Cor. 1:24

5

step. He says that Christ Himself is the wisdom of God. (See 1 Cor. 1:24.)

The personification of wisdom is not just a list of rules, important as they are, or a list of proverbs, or even a sacred book, necessary as it is. The personalization of wisdom reaches its climax in the Person of Jesus Christ who is the Wisdom of God. He is the key to the universe. If you apprehend Him you will be able to fit the pieces of life together.

Thus the Christian message moves beyond the wise proverbs of Solomon, which even commend themselves to the nonbeliever, and says that in the deepest sense the wisdom of God can only be found in the Person of Jesus Christ.

Wisdom is also an emotion. "The fear of the Lord is the beginning of knowledge" (Prov. 1:7, *NASB*). Some people say, "Well, haven't we got enough to fear? We have to fear the bomb—we have to fear disease—we have to fear war—we have to fear the economy—we have to fear death. I'm tired of religions that exploit and live on fear. Why is the fear of the Lord the beginning of knowledge?"

I can answer by saying that the word here is "to reverence." To fear the Lord, then, is to have reverence for God. Since God is the ultimate question, the fear of the Lord is actually a matter of ultimates, those things in life that concern us most. If there is a God and He is the author of the universe, then He is the only really important fact. Unless we concern ourselves with Him, and how we may know Him and His will, then we are indeed fools.

Look at medical science—how advanced it is—and all the lives that are saved. But we still die! What good is medical science without the ultimate question? What good is political science? What good are all of these things if we have missed the ultimate question? The agnostic says, "I don't know about God, so I'll just forget about the question and make it unimportant in my life." This is folly. It is to answer secondary questions and to ignore the primary.

To fear God is to take Him with ultimate seriousness. Even if you cannot be sure of the existence of God, you may have the ultimate concern. But you will never find God or the wisdom of God, which is Christ, until that concern becomes deep enough in your life to be called fear—the fear of the Lord, the beginning of all wisdom.

A friend of mine, a former college football player, the father of two children, was dying of cancer of the liver. As I looked at his jaundiced face and spoke with him for the last time, he said, "God has given me the years to see my children grow up." His daughter was crippled. As we sat there it was related that his wife had said, "Why did this have to happen to us? Why were we given first a handicapped child? And now, in the prime of life, why are you dying of cancer? Why?"

He had looked at her and said, "My dear, why *not* us? Why *not* us?"

During our visit, he told me, "I'm not afraid. I've seen my son grow to manhood; and though I fight depression, I stand so close to God now that I experience a joy I never experienced before. And if, to experience the peace I now feel I must endure these pains, then the pains are blessed."

Wise man! His experience of the fear of God conquered all these other fears. It is only when we fear what we ought to fear that we fear not at all. The fear of the Lord is the beginning of all wisdom.

Lord, as we begin our studies in the book of Proverbs, help us to be instructed by the wisdom of those short and pithy sentences. But help us to see, O God, that wisdom is ultimately personified in the Person of Jesus Christ. We must find wisdom not by memorizing proverbs but in the fear of the Lord that conquers all fear through Jesus Christ. Amen.

Trust in the Lord with all thine heart; and lean not unto thine own understanding. In all thy ways acknowledge him, and he shall direct thy paths.   **Proverbs 3:5,6**

POSTURES
OF
WISDOM

This is one of the famous passages committed to memory by Christian people. It has had a most significant role in the lives of both Jewish and Christian people. One of the ancient rabbis, Rabbi Bar Kappara, said that this passage is the text on which all the essential principles of Judaism hinge.[1] It summarizes the Old Testament.

And I think it speaks directly to our time. I don't know many people who are not deeply interested in finding guidance from God for their lives. This text promises that guidance. It gives three postures of wisdom which shall insure our finding the will of God.

The first of the postures is trust—"Trust in the Lord with all thine heart." Trust is familiar to most of us as one of the fundamental verbs of the Christian life, and because we use this term so generally in a religious sense we tend to isolate it from the rest of life. But trust is not only religious, it is an essential posture of life for all emotional soundness and even for survival. In the final analysis all government, all economics, all currency and banking, all institutions and all marriages, all relationships between people, are fundamentally governed by trust. Without trust, society deteriorates into paranoia, the feeling that everybody is out to get you.

The inability to trust not only means the collapse of government and of marriages and families, it is in itself a symptom of deep emotional illness. The famous psychoanalyst, Erik Erikson, says that the capacity to trust is the very foundation of emotional health.[2] He says it is essential that a person have confidence in his relationships with people so that meeting others is not a threat but an opportunity.

One must also affirm that life itself is not a conspiracy, but a friend and an ally. And Erikson says that unless a person can have this basic inward peace and confidence about life and its outcome, he will never achieve emotional maturity or wholeness.

Trust, then, is the capacity to rest in the confidence that people are with us and that the very universe is with us. But we know that there's an adder in

12

Eden—there's a snake in the grass. We have been betrayed. We have all experienced an unfriendly world in the form of tragedy and defeat. While we agree that a trusting attitude toward life and toward people is essential to our peace of mind, we also talk about that "trusting fool" who is unable to discern the diabolical schemes of those who would exploit him.

If you look to this life alone to affirm the necessity and the rightness of trust, you're foolish. What Erikson is saying indirectly, is: "There must be something beyond life that is reliable. I can't rely on nature—sometimes it sends too much rain and sometimes too little. I can't altogether rely on friends—sometimes they don't help me at all. Sometimes they help me too much!"

If trust is essential to human happiness Erikson is an indirect witness to the fact that beyond this life, is One in whom we may place our trust. "Trust in the Lord with all thine heart. . . ." What Erikson is saying, although he does not mean to say it, is simply this: There is no wholeness in life apart from trust in God and in His Son, Jesus Christ.

You say, "That's all very well. I acknowledge the Creed. I consider myself a Christian. And yet at times I just have this fear that catches hold of me and destroys my capacity to enjoy life. I worry. I'm obsessed with anxieties. I realize that, despite certain tragedies, things have worked out fairly well for me, but I'm still riddled by fear and anxieties. So for you to tell me to hang loose, relax, trust in God, that's all very beautiful. I just wish I could do it—but I can't."

A woman once came to me for help because she was so frightened she couldn't stand to be alone when her husband went to work. She would shake so badly that sometimes he would have to come home from work early.

She said, "I want to trust in God, but something just happens to me. I become frightened and I go to my good Christian friends and they say, 'Just trust the Lord.' Trust the Lord! I want to but I can't."

It sounds so simple—"Just trust the Lord." But the fact is, we have to come to a different understanding of the word "trust." Trusting is a habit, almost an unconscious attititude. You don't trust or half-trust, like turning on a water faucet.

Psalm 37 says, "Trust in the Lord, and do good. . . . Commit thy way unto the Lord; trust also in him; and he shall bring it to pass" (Ps. 37:3,5). There are two sides to the matter of trust. There is the decision of trust and the habit of trust. The first is called "commitment;" the second is called "trust." Trust follows commitment, not always right away, but it begins there. In the middle of our fears we make a *decision* to trust. This does not immediately bring the *habit* of trust, but if we will muster the courage to commit our way to God we shall soon learn to trust.

The wife of the pastor under whom I grew up once said, "My biggest problem in life is, I get down to pray with all my burdens and lay them all down to commit them all to the Lord. Then as I jump up off my knees I bring them all back to bed with me." But over the years she began to leave a few of them on the floor when she got up.

14

The very act of commitment begins to reinforce the habit. Just because you cannot rest completely, do not draw back from the commitment of the moment.

We sometimes make fun of individuals who keep responding to invitations to receive Christ or to re-dedicate their lives. We say, "Brother So-and-So has been saved five times in the last three years." I don't think we ought to mock such a person. He is having a tremendous problem with trust. There is nothing to be laughed at in his committing himself again, because it is in these serial commitments that he eventually grows into the posture of trust.

If your attitude toward life is not one of rest but of agitation, commit your way to God. You say, "I've done it before." Commit yourself again, not thinking that maybe this time it will work and God will accept you. He's already received you. But the road to the rest of faith is commitment—and commitment—and commitment—and commitment. There is no other road. You must *learn* to walk on it and to rest in it. But if you draw back in doubt from recommitting yourself to God you will never learn to rest in the posture called trust.

The second posture is "Lean not unto thine own understanding."

In our culture today we systematically try to build self-reliance. Parents try to bring a child to autonomy; society teaches us to manage our own affairs, to feed and clothe ourselves and run our lives.

Self-reliance becomes almost a form of religion at times. William Ernest Henley's defiant "Invictus" reacts against certain religious people who always talk about how helpless they are and how weak they are. He wants to let people know he's not a weakling. He says:

Out of the night that covers me,
Black as the Pit from pole to pole,
I thank whatever gods may be
For my unconquerable soul . . .
It matters not how strait the gate,
How charged with punishments the scroll,
I am the master of my fate;
I am the captain of my soul.[3]

But what does the wise king of Israel say? "Trust in the Lord with all thine heart; and lean not unto thine own understanding." There is a limit to self-reliance.

Jeremiah, the great prophet, was no weakling, but he illustrates the principle of trusting God. He stood against the whole nation when the Babylonians and all the enemies of Judah were coming down from the north. He told his people not to resist. He told them that defeat by these enemies was the judgment of God upon them and that it was useless to oppose Nebuchadnezzar.

Every time Nebuchadnezzar would come down and conquer Judah and then leave with his army, a bunch of the nationalists would rebel and try to set up an independent state. Jeremiah would say, "No! If you do it you will be destroyed." Soon the clouds would be seen in the distance and Nebuchadnezzar would be back. This happened four times before the people of Judah finally gave up. Jeremiah was a man who singlehandedly spoke against the folly of Judah's defiance of Nebuchadnezzar.

What does Jeremiah say about trust? How does he find this inner poise to stand against the whole nation and against the kings, and to endure prison? "O Lord, I know that the way of man is not in himself: it is not in man that walketh to direct his steps" (Jer. 10:23).

Henley could write great poetry, but Jeremiah could do great and heroic deeds simply because he knew his real strength lay not in self-reliance but in trusting God. If a man feels that he has made it on his own he is ultimately a fool—he is only one heartbeat from death.

There was a farmer who didn't have enough sense to sell out. He bought a field upon which nothing could be raised. The soil was infertile. He nearly starved to death. One day somebody came by with a paper the farmer didn't understand and said, "You might get some money for this someday." So he signed it, and they drilled and struck an oil gusher.

Immediately the farmer moved to the city and became one of the leaders of society, an authority on economics, business, education, politics, everything. He said, "I'm a self-made man." There's an old Swedish proverb that declares the same principle: "It's always the dumbest farmers that raise the biggest potatoes."

Many of the good things that happen to us are really not as much the result of our cleverness as they are a result of the providence of God. And some of the long shots that people take, where the chances are a hundred-to-one, only a fool would take. But the man is too dumb to know that, so he takes the chance and he makes it. He's successful not because he's smart, but because he's dumb and the odds are with him for once. But it soon catches up.

My father tells about a bookkeeper who used to work for him. He was fifty-five years old; he had worked all of his life, and he had saved fifteen thousand dollars for his retirement. "But," he thought, "this isn't very much to retire on. I think I'm going to invest it in the market."

So he went out and put his money in the market. Within ninety days it was worth fifty thousand dollars. The man came to my father and said, "Look what I've done!"

And Father said, "Now be careful. This is what you've saved for your retirement."

"Well," the man replied, "if I was successful the last time . . ." So he went out and he did it again! He was soon worth seventy thousand dollars. Four months later he came in and resigned because his money had grown to one hundred thousand dollars. He was going to go into the market as a speculator. A year later, he came back with a diamond stickpin in his tie and carrying a diamond-studded cane. He told my dad, "Well, you have very limited judgment." About this time my father was beginning to wonder whether his former employee may have been right.

Four months later the man came back and asked for his job. All he could say was, "I haven't got a dime."

The tragedy of arrogance is not only that it alienates

us from people and makes us unpopular, but also that it is foolishness. If we are indeed to survive in life we must have the honesty to admit our frailties and our ignorance and to lean, not on ourselves, but upon God.

The third posture is, "In all your ways acknowledge Him." You ask, "How does that become a posture?" It is the posture of wholeheartedness. If you are going to rest on God, then rest all the way.

"In all your ways acknowledge Him, and He shall direct your paths." One of the problems we have in trying to discern the Lord's will is that guidance comes not through something written on the wall or through some other source, but through inner awareness. Now the trouble with inner awareness is that we have many impulses and most of them are anonymous. God doesn't come to us and say, "This is God speaking. Go and do this." And when the devil enters our consciousness he doesn't say, "This is the devil speaking; please do thus and so." It doesn't happen that way.

Abraham Lincoln received letters from many people telling him God's will for ending the Civil War. On one occasion he responded: "I hope it will not be irreverent of me to say that if God would reveal His will to others on a point so connected with my duty . . . it might be supposed He would reveal it to me; for unless I am more deceived in myself than I often am, it is my earnest desire to know the will of Providence in this matter."[4] But a clear revelation was beyond his expectation.

God's will is never an easy matter. A man came

to me one day and said, "I got a revelation from God."

"What's that?" I said.

"He told me to leave my wife."

"How do you know?" I replied.

"Well, I got peace in my heart about it."

It doesn't work that way. How do you know the difference between the voice of God and the voice of the devil? It's seldom an easy matter.

The way to be assured of God's direction, the Bible says, is to acknowledge Him "wholeheartedly." In *all* your ways make Him Lord. There is no other way. God withdraws Himself from a divided heart. Furthermore, when we sense that we are disobedient, that elements of our life are apart from Him, we avoid God. Then we do not hear His voice. His guidance is not available for our conscience.

Scientists sometimes find that an experiment which is supposed to work a certain way according to their theories doesn't work out. Then they postulate what they call an intervening variable; there's something gumming up the works. Some other factor has crept in. The reason that some of us seem always so confused about the divine will of God is that there is an intervening variable called self-will—it is an area of our lives where Jesus Christ is not Lord, an area of disobedience. This self-will destroys any capacity for us to discern the divine will.

A half-hearted Christian is probably a more miserable person than one who is not a Christian at all. A nonbeliever can organize life around his own selfish desires and can achieve a passable, functioning structure. He can put his life together on that basis. But

20

if a person divides his life in two, so that part of his allegiance is to God and part is to himself, he's going to introduce two warring elements into his consciousness. Guilt, hostility and conflict will result.

This divided allegiance is one of the leading causes of nervous breakdown among Christian people. You want God's will? You must want it wholeheartedly; that is the only way. When you are wholehearted, you can learn to rest.

George MacDonald was a nineteenth century Scottish preacher and novelist. He was the man who influenced the famous writer, C. S. Lewis, the most. MacDonald was put out of his church because he had some problems with aspects of the Westminster Confession of the Church of Scotland. He lived most of his life in total poverty. He could scarcely find a job and was unable to earn a living as a novelist until he was quite old.

This is what he said about finding the will, and the rest, of God: "This is the sane, wholesome and practical fact: first, that it is a man's business to do the will of God; second, that God takes on Himself the special care of that man; and third, therefore that man ought never to be afraid of anything."[5] Here was a man who had a lot of suffering in his life, but who had learned not to be afraid because he stood in the posture of wholeheartedness.

The Civil War general, William Tecumseh Sherman, dearly loved his wife. When she died, he wrote to DeWitt Talmadge, the famous preacher, "I am sure that you know that the God who created the minnow, and who has molded the rose and the carnation giving each its sweet fragrance, will provide for those mortal men who strive to do right in this world which He himself has stocked with birds, animals and men. At all events I will trust Him with absolute confidence."[6]

O God, teach us what commitment and trust means and then enable us to practice daily putting that trust into action. Keep us from relying on our own abilities but lead us to rely wholeheartedly on You. Amen

footnotes

1. Israel Goldstein, *Toward a Solution* (New York: Putnam, 1940), p. 45.

2. Erik H. Erikson, *Childhood and Society* (New York: W. W. Norton and Co., 1950), pp. 24ff.

3. James D. Morrison, ed., *Masterpieces of Religious Verse* (New York: Harper and Row, Publishers, 1948), pp. 575,576.

4. Archer Shaw, ed. and comp., "Reply to Chicago Church Committee," Sept. 13, 1862, VII, 29, *The Lincoln Encyclopedia* (New York: The Macmillan Co., 1920), p. 282.

5. C. S. Lewis, ed., *George MacDonald: An Anthology* (New York: The Macmillan Co., 1947).

6. Lloyd Lewis, *Sherman, Fighting Prophet* (New York: Harcourt and Brace, 1932), p. 649.

Don't be conceited, sure of your own wisdom. Instead, trust and reverence the Lord, and turn your back on evil; when you do that, then you will be given renewed health and vitality.

Honor the Lord by giving him the first part of all your income, and he will fill your barns with wheat and barley and overflow your wine vats with the finest wines.

Young man, do not resent it when God chastens and corrects you, for his punishment is proof of his love. Just as a father punishes a son he delights in to make him better, so the Lord corrects you.

Proverbs 3:7-12, *TLB*

FACETS
OF
WISDOM

Wisdom, like a diamond, has many colorful facets. You can look at it from any angle and see something different. In this section of Proverbs we want to examine three specific facets of wisdom: the facet of humility, "Don't be conceited, sure of your own wisdom"; the facet of generosity, "Honor the Lord by giving him the first part of all your income"; and the facet of submission, "Do not resent it when God chastens and corrects you."

Let us look first at the facet of humility. "Don't be conceited, sure of your own wisdom. Instead, trust and reverence the Lord, and turn your back on evil" (Prov. 3:7). No wise man is ever arrogant. As a matter of fact, arrogance is the giveaway, the telltale symptom of ignorance. Pride is a form of ignorance and is never found in wise men. That's why no wise man ever tells you that he is wise. The wisest of all men reflects the Socratic spirit: "I know that I am not wise."

I recall a young student running into me one day and saying, "Pastor, I've just enrolled in college and I am so excited with my new history professor. He says there has never been a proper textbook written on American history and therefore there is no assigned reading in this course. He is going to set us straight."

And I said, "This hasn't happened since Socrates. I regret that at Yale, Harvard, Oxford and Cambridge they still have to rely on these outmoded and inaccurate textbooks, but Socrates has returned to the classroom in a twentieth century junior college. When does he speak next time? I want to come and hear him bray." The very arrogance of the posture demonstrated the inadequacy of the teacher. "No one has ever seen it right before but *I* have now seen it."

But arrogance is not found only in the classroom. Kenneth Cauthen lists the sage advice of some of the alleged wise men of yesteryear, men wise in their own ideas. The famed surgeon, Alfred Zelto, wrote in 1839, "The abolishment of pain in surgery is a chimera. It is absurd to go on seeking it today." That was before ether.

Harper's Weekly said in 1902: "The actual building of roads devoted to motorcars is not for the near future in spite of many rumors to that effect." Have you ridden on one of those lately?

And in 1945 no less a scholar than Vannevar Bush commented to President Truman as follows, regarding the atomic bomb, "The bomb will never go off, and I speak as an expert on explosives."

Or consider the remark of the *New York Times*. One week before the successful flight of the Wright brothers in Kitty Hawk, North Carolina, they commented about a rival plane builder who was trying to build a heavier-than-air machine, "We hope that Professor Langley will not put his substantial greatness as a scientist in further peril by continuing to waste his time, and the money involved, in further airship experiments. Life is short and he is capable of services to humanity incomparably greater than can be expected to result from trying to fly."

Back a few centuries a special commission of wise men was set up by King Ferdinand and Queen Isabella of Spain to comment upon the wisdom of giving money to one Christopher Columbus to sail west in an attempt to reach Asia. The committee reported in 1490 that the proposed voyage was a waste of money and a mistake. Their reasons were: first, the voyage to Asia would require three years. Second, the Western Ocean is infinite and perhaps unnavigable. Third, if he reached the Antipodes he would not be able to get back. Fourth, there are no Antipodes because the greater part of the globe is covered with water and because St. Augustine said so. Fifth, of the five zones, only three are habitable. Sixth, so many centuries after the Creation it is unlikely that anyone could find hitherto unknown lands of any value.[1] So has been the advice through the centuries of men wise in their own eyes. They are the fools that history remembers.

Let me probe a bit deeper. The wisdom of Proverbs is not a scientific evaluation of the possible or the impossible, but a spiritual directive to obedience. "Do

27

not be wise in your own eyes; fear the Lord and turn away from evil" (Prov. 3:7, *NASB*).

The great ethical efforts of our time have been striving to make indicative statements out of the divine imperatives. Now what does that mean? Translated into barefoot language, it means trying to give a rational and persuasive explanation to every one of God's commandments.

As far as possible, it's good to show that God's commands are not foolish or unreasonable. But we may be tricked into assuming that we need to obey only when we can see the prudence of the command. This is the error of a school of thought called utilitarianism which claims that the good can only be judged by the consequences. According to this theory, when it appears that one of the commandments of God will produce adverse or unhappy consequences, we may suspend the commandment.

The Bible certainly enjoins us to consider the consequences of how we act. But who really knows all the consequences of an act? An act, once committed, has an infinite, unending series of consequences which we cannot measure in this unpredictable world. To define right and wrong by your understanding of the consequences is to assume that you are infinite in your understanding.

Or if we may move to a more modern ethical theory, take the "new morality" as expounded by Joseph Fletcher of the Episcopal Theological Seminary in Cambridge. Fletcher says, "The situationist enters into every decision-making situation fully armed with the ethical maxims of his community and its heritage, and he treats them with respect as illuminators of his problems. Just the same he is prepared in any situation to compromise them or set them aside *in the situation* if love seems better served by doing so."[2] He recognizes that we can't make the decision in terms of consequences, so he simply says to do whatever is the loving thing at the moment. Of course, he never adequately defines love. He has not plumbed the depths of human understanding or understood man's capacity for self-deception and rationalization.

What selfishness, and even perversity, has been baptized with the name of love! We need to see, in all humility and light, that while it may appear to be foolish to be obedient, we are not the ultimate measure. If God says, "Thou shalt not," then thou shalt not!

Or put the emphasis the other way around. We are prey, to some extent, to succumbing to the modern advice-givers about child-rearing. They say, "Never tell a child just to go do something. You always have to explain why." This is generally sound advice. You can surely get more cooperation that way and it develops a relationship of trust. But the child at times must be compelled to act simply because the command has come, without understanding why.

The great heroes of the faith have been those who obeyed because God had commanded, not because they understood. The proud assumption in so many of us, and the very thing that betrays us, is the conclusion that we've reached maturity and we can handle any situation on our own. The teen-ager who wants to experiment with drugs says, "Well, I see a lot of people doing it. I don't see that much harm in it. It isn't going to hurt me. I can handle it."

It is the same argument in terms of alcohol. "We're over eighteen (or twenty-one). We're mature, we know how to handle it." Surely you do! If you've been reading the statistics lately, your odds aren't so good. Mature people don't seem to be able to handle alcohol so well. I have heard many tragic confessions and sobs in my study from people in my congregation who thought they were mature enough to handle alcohol. If anything brings the fires of hell and its torment into this life it is a problem with alcohol or drugs. In our sensate, pleasure-oriented society how many of us think we can play with fire and not be burned? The wise man says, "I don't think I'm strong enough to play with that." The first facet of wisdom is humility.

A second facet is generosity. "Honour the Lord with thy substance, and with the firstfruits of all thine increase: so shall thy barns be filled with plenty, and the presses shall burst out with new wine" (Prov. 3:9,10).

There are two kinds of faith, "head faith"—what we *say* we believe, and "visceral faith"—what we *really* believe. I remember being struck with the significant difference between these two kinds of faith on a plane ride to Los Angeles from San Francisco. I was in seminary then. That was in the days of the old DC3's and DC4's, the unpressurized planes where you were afraid the wires were going to break and the wing was going to fall off. When they came in low over the San Gabriel Mountains, the wings really flapped.

I was reading a book on theology when a most lovely young stewardess sat down next to me and began to question me about my faith and to talk about her fears. I said, "If you have faith you don't need to be afraid. I put myself into the hands of God." Just then we started hitting the airpockets over the San Gabriels and I froze. That ended our conversation. She had the funniest look when she walked away. It struck me at that instant that there's a vast difference between head faith and visceral faith.

The tragedy with many people is not that they don't claim to have God in their lives, but that, while they claim to have Him, they still don't trust Him. The most significant telltale symptom of this lack of trust is that they never get around to honoring the Lord with their substance. We've got to make sure that the family has security; and we don't add to the security by whopping off a hunk of it and putting it in the offering plate, unless we really believe that *God* is our security.

As I thought about this the name of Abraham crossed my mind. Abraham was one of the "biggies" when it comes to the life of visceral faith.

Abraham learned that generosity and integrity came before his economic security. You remember that little scene with Abraham (when he was still Abram) and his nephew Lot. Because their herdsmen were having a conflict, they agreed to separate. One of them would have to live down in the valley, one of them would have to dwell up on the mountain. Uncle Abram, who should have had the seniority, said, "Lot, you choose. Take whatever you want." Lot looked up at the rocky slopes and the sparsely scattered grass of the mountain. He began to consider the mortality rate of his sheep falling down the canyons and the danger from the coyotes and the wolves; then he looked over the fat watered plains, the waist-high grass, and said, "That's pretty good."

Lot also saw the glistening roofs of Sodom, including the tower which was the symbol of the great University of Sodom, and he said, "Culture and education for my children—since you, Uncle Abe, don't even have a son yet—for the sake of my children, I've really got to have this."

So he took it. The only trouble was, everybody else wanted it, too. Soon every vagabond, every marauding tribe swept down to burn, to loot and to pillage. They eventually took Lot prisoner. And Lot, who thought the fundamental structure of his life was economic gain and cultural advantage for his children, discovered not only that he was in physical jeopardy, but also that his children had been corrupted and destroyed in Sodom.

Can that happen in your town today? You say, "But I've always tried to put church and God in my life. I've wanted the best for my family." But have you put it together in the right order?

Abraham is up there in land nobody wants—but he finds that every rock is a fort. He's the one who finally rescues Lot. And when the battles are over and Lot is safe, Abraham goes to Melchizedek, king of Salem, a priest of God, and gives a tithe of all he possesses. The key to the survival of Abraham was his trust in God and the fact that he honored God with his substance.

Finally, we have the facet of submission. The tenth verse closes with the statement, "So shall thy barns be filled with plenty, and thy presses shall burst out with new wine." The Bible is not naïve. It is true that when a man takes care of his obligation to God, God takes care of him. But another verse follows which recognizes that God's care does not always come in the form of material blessings: "My son, despise not the chastening of the Lord; neither be weary of his correction: for whom the Lord loveth he correcteth; even as a father the son in whom he delighteth" (Prov. 3:11,12).

Many devout men have become poor, but this is not necessarily a sign that they are filled with folly or that they are unspiritual. God sees that there is a measure of suffering in life which we must all experience if we are to grow.

Our culture has taught us falsely that the only evil is pain. However, pain is *not* an ultimate evil. It is an enemy, true, but it can be made a slave, captured and enlisted in the cause of goodness. The very instance of suffering may be a sign of God's love, rather than of His disfavor. Hear the words of the poet:

> I walked a mile with Pleasure.
> She chattered all the way,
> But left me none the wiser
> For all she had to say.
>
> I walked a mile with Sorrow,
> And ne'er a word said she;
> But, oh, the things I learned from her
> When Sorrow walked with me![3]

It is often in our suffering that we grow the most. Youth gives us idealism, vigor, and beauty; but I know from my own life that youth tends to have a harsh, metallic arrogance. I see it not only in the young people of today; I still see some of it in myself. Only suffering can humanize and take away this sort of attitude.

David was a man of action as well as a man of deep feeling. He could thunder against his enemies with frightening zeal. But you really don't stand close to the center of David's life until you see a David broken by his sinfulness or until you see a David broken by the rebellion of his own son.

God always loves us; and the writer to the Hebrews says God can succor us, He can strengthen us, because He suffered. Suffering even did something in the life of the omnipotent deity, in the life of Christ.

And in your life there is nothing that will make you more tender toward others, and less judgmental, than sin and failure which has broken you.

Christians can be very unlovely people, particularly when filled with moral indignation. Our eloquent denunciation of the iniquities around us do not make us beautiful. But when our hearts have been broken in sorrow over one child whom we love, we become beautiful. That is the beauty of Jesus Christ, a loving heart broken over a wayward child, a daughter or son. "Despise not the chastening of the Lord."

Oh, Lord, if suffering must come, grant us the wisdom to see it remaking us into beings mirroring the beauty of Jesus. Amen.

1. Gerald Kennedy quoting from Kenneth Cauthen's *Christian Biopolitics* (Nashville: Abingdon Press, 1971) in "The Starting Line," *Pulpit Digest* vol. 53, no. 391, Jan. 1972, p. 60.

2. Joseph Fletcher, *Situation Ethics* (Philadelphia: Westminster Press, 1966), p. 26.

3. Robert Browning Hamilton, from "Along the Road," in *Familiar Quotations,* ed. John Bartlett, 13th edition (Boston: Little, Brown and Co., 1956), p. 907.

Let your manhood be a blessing; rejoice in the wife of your youth. Let her charms and tender embrace satisfy you. Let her love alone fill you with delight.

Proverbs 5:18,19, *TLB*

WISDOM
AND
CHASTITY

I do not suppose that there has been any time in the past century when the Christian understanding and teaching concerning the sexual passions have been under such overt attack. The secular community has accused Christianity's strong sexual code of being against sex. The teaching that the sexual relationship must be confined to marriage is called puritanical. Even within the confines of the Christian community, that portion of the church which has forsaken the ethical teachings of the Scriptures and given rise to the "new morality" criticizes the biblical stand on chastity.

Of more concern even than the ideological attack

is what is happening in practice in our society. We think of the free morality of today's young people, but let me hasten to add that I am not at all sure that there is more unchastity at an anti-war march than at an American Legion convention. I spend more time counseling adults in middle life who are having problems of infidelity and unchastity than I spend counseling young people in these areas. This is not just the sin of teen-agers.

Proverbs 5:1-14 describes the destiny of sexual relationships outside of marriage. They are described as fundamentally destructive. The second half of the chapter is given to the description of how fulfilling the sexual relationship can be within marriage. No honest scholar who reads this passage describing the joy of the relationship of husband and wife together can honestly conclude that the Hebrew/Christian tradition is anti-sexual. The sexual code is strong not because sex is looked upon as something evil, but because it is looked upon as something sublime. It is only because we think so highly of sex that we address such ethical attention to it.

Now lest some people discount it by saying, "Well with the advent of antibiotics and the pill, there is no longer any reason to abide by these teachings," let me say that such an attitude betrays a very shallow understanding of the meaning of sexuality. To understand sexuality properly, we will have to take a profound look at what life is really about.

First, we must look at love as relationship. Life is relationship. That is a very fundamental premise. To be is to be in relation to someone—to be in relationship to a spouse, to children, to parents, to friends, to associates, to God. That's the fundamental concept of relationships.

From the very first chapter of Genesis we discover almost a divine loneliness, a divine longing to be in relationship. God said, "Let us make man" (Gen. 1:26). God sought relationships. Strange as it may seem, there is almost an incompleteness in the divine solitude. We don't really understand the meaning of the phrase "God is love" (1 John 4:8) until we understand that life is fundamentally relationships. And plenitude of relationship is fullness of life. Paucity of relationship is impoverishment of life.

Thus when God creates Adam, He says, "It is not good for the man to be alone" (Gen. 2:18, *NASB*). For to be is to be in relationship. The ordination of marriage is given to us in Genesis and reaffirmed to us by our Lord—"And the two shall be one flesh." The sexual union as the highest form of human relationship.

Then we come to the apostle Paul, who is often accused of thinking sex so terrible. Let us be honest in our scholarship. He says not only that sex is good, but that it is the only human relationship that begins to measure adequately the relationship between God and the believer. You can't get a higher view of sex than that. (See Eph. 5:21–33.)

The newer forms of psychiatry and psychology are turning away from looking at mental health and mental illness in terms of a solitary individual; they are now defining mental health or mental illness in terms of relationship. We define a person in terms of his adequacy in relationships. This "new" thinking reflects the Hebrew/Christian understanding in a better measure than did the old psychology, for it recognizes that *to be* is fundamentally to be in relationship.

That leads to another interesting axiom: relationships are vulnerable. If you're going to be in relationship with someone, you have an infinite capacity to hurt and to be hurt. The closer the relationship, the greater the vulnerability and the capacity to hurt.

Thus, in the relationship between parents and children, which is so close, there is an infinite capacity to bless or to destroy. And the same is true between husband and wife, and even between God and man.

Someone said that mankind is like a herd of porcupines at the North Pole. They're so cold in their isolation that they move together. When they come together they stick and hurt each other so they move apart. They keep moving until they are too cold, then they come together for warmth and they get hurt. Then they move apart again. This is a description of what we mean about the sublime and the painful in the matter of relationships.

Since pain is inevitable, integrity is all-important in relationship. Just look at literature and see how much it is preoccupied with the love story, and with the pain that love brings. Look at any love story, any soap opera on TV. Listen to music. The blues are generally laments showing feelings of hurt; they reflect strong feeling of love but the hurt is also there because the love has been broken.

If to be is to be in relationship, and relationship means vulnerability, then love is the only right relationship. That is where the person in relationship to another looks upon the welfare and happiness of his

40

partner as more important than his own. God is love. Anyone who uses the word "love" selfishly, who does not put the happiness of the partner ahead of his own, is giving more pain than pleasure. Such a relationship is fundamentally exploitive and destructive. True love is a willingness to suffer that the other might achieve happiness.

We see this selflessness in God who is love. We see it in Christ, who was delivered up for our sins, suffering in our behalf. "Greater love hath no man than this, that a man lay down his life for his friends" (John 15:13). And Jesus laid down His life for us. He endured the ultimate sacrifice.

If we understand relationship as a fundamental fact of life, and take into account our capacity to hurt each other, we find that love is the only satisfying kind of relationship. And we also find that part of love is suffering for the welfare of others.

The sexual relationship which can bring such satisfaction and happiness to life is also the relationship, more than any other, that can bring unhappiness and suffering. This is why the Bible insists that sexual relationships can never take place apart from love as God defines it. That's why the Bible so strongly says sexual relationships can never be casual. They must always be in the context of love.

Some people feel sex can be safely enjoyed outside of marriage, providing both parties understand that it is nothing more nor less than a physical act. Such language is naïve; inevitably it is more than that.

Love is not only the right relationship, love is faithfulness. One who really loves another more than he loves himself is concerned not only with that person's

41

welfare today, but also with that person's welfare tomorrow. When people enter into the sexual relationship because of love, the question is "You love me as I am today in my physical prime, but will you love me tomorrow when that is no longer true?" I'm well aware at thirty-eight that I am not as beautiful as I used to be, which is assuming a great deal about what I used to be. When I'm to be loved, I'm to be loved as a whole person. Any love that's not committed to the future is not love. I am my tomorrow as well as my today, and to say "I only love you today" is to say "I don't love all of you." It is to say "I'll make up my mind about you tomorrow."

When someone says, "I love you today, but I'm not going to talk about tomorrow as I might change my mind," is less than loving. It is the telltale symptom of selfishness and exploitation, not of love.

God is faithful. If you understand God's love you will understand why faithfulness is an attribute of God. God says, "No matter what happens I won't let you down. I will always keep you. I will always care for you."

Our society has cast aside this concept of faithfulness not just in the marriage or sexual relationships, but in all relationships. The good life is assumed to be prosperity, peace of mind, or lots of kicks. The Hebrews, on the other hand, said it didn't matter if you suffered a lot, and it didn't matter ultimately if you were poor or whether you had a good education, or whether you were famous, or whether you had good physical health. The question was "Were you a faithful person?" It wasn't whether or not you'd had a good life. What happened to you in life from

42

the outside didn't ultimately matter. What mattered was your faithfulness in your relationships to God and to your fellowman. Love cannot be love unless it has faithfulness in it.

Finally, love is a covenant—a covenant of faithfulness. This is really the thing that you have to understand about the Old Testament and the New Testament; it is what underlies all ethics, all human behavior and the relationship of God and man, and man and man, and man and woman. All love must be covenant love.

You recall one of the first covenants of the Old Testament: God said to Abraham, "I am going to make of you a great nation, and I'm going to make your seed as the stars of heaven so that you can't even number them."

And Abraham said, "You know, God, in case You hadn't noticed, I'm a little older than I used to be. And God, I don't want to be indiscreet about it, but my wife and I are beyond any physical capacity to bear children" (see Gen. 17).

God said, "I am faithful. I have promised this to you." Abraham believed, and God counted it to him for righteousness. That is the great covenant with Abraham, which is the founding of the Jewish nation. And because it was a covenant of faith brought to pass by a miracle of God's grace, it becomes the foundation of our understanding of all relationship.

God's covenant with Israel is reaffirmed again and again through the pages of Scripture. God is faithful. Israel isn't faithful. The children of Israel keep breaking the covenants, and God punishes them. They run away. And God says, "I'm going to redeem you. I'm going to make you into the kind of people who will keep the covenant." God keeps His covenants, even though they are broken from the other side.

God's covenant is one of the great themes of the prophets. The relationship between Israel and Jehovah is most often pictured as the relationship between a husband and a wife. Israel becomes the wayward, unfaithful wife who commits adultery. But God is still faithful to His covenant.

God's covenant is a covenant of love. If there is love that transcends one's own interest, and if part of love is faithfulness, then this love means a commitment. This is where the word commitment really comes into the whole Christian understanding. It is an oath, a perpetual, unbreakable, irrevocable oath. God says, "I will never break My covenant. You can count on it. I will be your God."

Further, it was a public covenant. God says, "I make this covenant before all nations, and if I break it, I will break it in the eyes of all men. There are no secret arrangements. There is no shame. I am proud of this relationship. And I am willing to be accountable for it before every man and woman alive." It is unbreakable. Perpetual, public, unbreakable.

This is what a marriage ceremony is—a covenant. A lot of people say, "What's a marriage ceremony? Just fifteen minutes of time, a little document filed with the county clerk, and a piece of paper hung on the wall. What does it mean? It's not worth the paper it's written on."

Wait a minute. If you understand that life is fundamentally relationships, and the only ethical relationship is love, and love is faithfulness, then that covenant is the most sacred thing in your life.

I have often counseled with young people who say, "Pastor, you know, we're deeply in love. How can it be wrong to live together in sexual union?"

I say, "Do you really love each other?"

"Yes, we do."

"Do you intend to break this thing up if either of you are disappointed in each—"

"Oh, no, we really love each other."

"Are you ashamed of the fact that you love each other? Or are you willing to take a public oath to that effect?"

"What do you mean?"

"Well, it's called a wedding."

"Oh, no, no. We can't do that."

"Well, quit being hypocrites, and don't use the name of love. It's hypocrisy. If you really love, you will enter into covenant. Anything less is exploitation."

Charles A. Reich in *The Greening of America* says young people today don't want any of these entangling relationships. They just want to be free to love.[1] What he's really saying is, "We don't want love; we want to return to the jungle law of personal exploitation." He doesn't think he's saying that, but that is in effect what he is saying. There is no "free love"— only free exploitation. There is no love beyond fidelity to covenant.

Alvin Toffler, in his book *Future Shock*, describes marriages of tomorrow that will allow husbands and wives to discard each other in a simple procedure when they have "outgrown" each other.[2] I don't know how that can ever be simple. He is certainly revealing a very shallow understanding of human relationships.

How sublime rather is the Hebrew-Christian understanding of *love as covenant*. If we could recover this sense of fidelity as the foundation of marriage, the family would recover its healing and stabilizing role in modern society. In the Swedish story, *Vardag Sjamning*, Karl-Gustaf Hildebrand pictures an older couple musing about their life together. My friend Herbert Palmquist has translated their words:

"Perhaps they will not say of us: 'This was a happy marriage, they were examples for the rest of us. It was summer to live in their home.' But I want that one shall be able to say other words, simpler, but perhaps fully as great: 'They were honorable, they held out to the end. It is no disgrace for the hard granite to rest upon their graves'." Fidelity, not simply ecstatic infatuation, is the measure of authentic love.

Ultimately, it is by your covenants and your faithfulness to those covenants that you are going to be judged. That's the only important thing in your life. Yet all of us know too well that many times we fail to keep our part of the covenants we make with others and with God. The story of Israel's unfaithfulness is also the story of God being so faithful to His covenants that He forgives. That's what the gospel is all about. God is so faithful to His covenants that He will forgive you for your unfaithfulness.

This concept of covenant love and relationship is so basic that it not only offers the pattern for marriage, but it's the whole basis of what it means to be a Christian. When we talk about accepting Christ, or committing ourselves to Christ, we mean nothing more nor less than entering a covenant with Christ.

It can be very simple. A simple prayer like "Lord, help," can be a commitment of covenant. That relationship of covenant is from the very heart of God Himself; it is at the very heart of our lives, the heart of marriage, the heart of all family relationships. It is the very heart and basis of our salvation and hope of everlasting life.

Dear Father, we thank You for the gift of relationships and for the gift of sexuality and the sublime way that You have likened it to the relationship between Christ and His Church. We recognize that the strong teachings of Scripture about its use come not because it is evil but because it is good. Help us to see, O God, that these things can never take place apart from love, and love is always and without exception faithful. Through Jesus Christ, our Lord. Amen.

footnotes

1. Charles A. Reich, *Greening of America: How the Youth Culture Is Trying to Make America Liveable* (New York: Bantam Books, Inc., 1971), p. 245.

2. Alvin Toffler, *Future Shock* (New York: Bantam Books, Inc., 1971), pp. 251–253.

Take a lesson from the ants, you lazy fellow. Learn from their ways and be wise! For though they have no king to make them work, yet they labor hard all summer, gathering food for the winter.

Proverbs 6:6-8, *TLB*

WISDOM
AND
DEFERRED
PLEASURE

Wisdom and passion must be properly related, whether we think in the religious or the secular sense, for passion has always been a problem. Desire—physical, emotional, spiritual—is the energy that drives and motivates us to all action.

In an infant there is a desire for instant gratification. This is, in part, because the infant is helpless. However, all of us still have a certain desire for instant gratification. When we think of passion we think not only of appetite for food, or thirst for liquid, or sexual passion: we can also think of the passion for rest or for sleep. Sometimes that's the driving passion, especially on a Sunday morning. And we can think of the appetite for power, for wealth, for approval, for affection. These all represent passion, or a desire of the soul.

Many of us are inclined to feel that passion is an evil thing; but that is never a Hebrew or a Christian understanding of the meaning of the word. Hunger for God Himself is in fact a passion and a desire.

So passion in itself is neither good nor bad. Good or bad has to do rather with the ordering of the passions and the priority of the passions. Classical philosophy gives us the doctrine of deferred satisfaction: the idea that we must defer the satisfaction of some appetites in order to achieve our more important goals in life.

We see this in the animal kingdom. The ant doesn't spend all of his time eating; he spends a good deal of his time running back and forth carrying food into his nest so that he can survive the winter when there is no food. Thus the writer of the Proverbs tells a man who wants to sleep all day and doesn't want to work, "Go to the ant, thou sluggard; consider her ways and be wise" (Prov. 6:6).

The first step in coming to maturity is to develop a concept of deferred satisfaction. You must learn to deny yourself some things now in order to gain a more important fulfillment in the future. This is not only the law of maturation, it is the law of civilization. Instant gratification is the law of the jungle; civilization is conceived of as a way of organizing society by the regulation of law, denying people the instant gratification of helping themselves to their neighbors' goods and property in order to satisfy their own desires. Thus the individual may live a life of peace and quiet. And the stability of the society may provide a combination of goods and services which will meet the greatest good of the greatest number of people.

We see the law of deferred satisfaction operative in the disciplines of education and the disciplines of athletics. Young men will get out in the middle of summer, in ninety-seven degree temperatures, and torture themselves on an athletic field in order to become prolific at passing a pigskin across a hundred yards of cow pasture. You can't tell me that all this anguish and grunting and gasping and pain is unmitigated pleasure. But it demonstrates the doctrine of deferred satisfaction. We are willing to endure suffering now to get ready to win the game. The anguish of discipline and training is far outweighed by the triumph of winning.

The principle of deferred satisfaction breaks down in any society where we have immature people. We may call them criminal or emotionally disturbed. There is an element of both in most human behavior problems—both sin and sickness. One of the problems with the criminal mind, as the criminologist describes it to us, is that it does not have any real grasp of the concept of deferred satisfaction. These people are unable to weigh the fact that the satisfaction of their desire today by stealing another man's piece of property is very small compared to the risk of spending the next five years in prison.

This becomes very common among delinquent young people. You see it most vividly in the chronic repeater who seems totally unable to connect what he does and the consequences that will follow. He is not a free man; he is totally a slave of the impulse of the moment. And we have the kleptomaniac, the person who knows he may go to jail, but who cannot resist stealing something. He is totally victimized by his drive to satisfy this passion right now.

We read many case histories of young men who have gone to prison for stealing automobiles and two days after they're out they steal another car. They get another ten years, and when that's up, on the way home they steal another car. They never get home. The simple impulse to steal an automobile is so strong that they have absolutely no capacity to resist or to think through the consequences.

In much popular thinking today, in the revolt against the concept of the disciplined life and in the revolt against what is called the puritan ethic, many people are now saying that we *are* to gratify our desires instantly. We are to do our thing in the moment without worrying about the consequence tomorrow. This popular concept that everyone is supposed to do his own thing, whatever happens to appeal to him at the moment, has tended to spread a grievous sickness in our society.

The idea of deferred satisfaction is not a uniquely Christian idea. It was recognized by reflective men throughout history. It was described by Plato, more than two thousand years ago. Socrates tells of the two horses and the chariot. There was a black horse and a white horse: one was passion and the other was reason, and they fought against each other. It was only as the person, riding in the chariot, could make the horse of reason dominate the horse of passion that the chariot could get anywhere at all.

In that story we see the regulation of the passions by rationality, the real thrust of Greek philosophy; and of course, philosophy, by definition, is the love of wisdom, which brings us right back to the book of Proverbs. When you develop a desire for the rational regulation of passion, a desire which is strong enough to overcome any individual appetite, you will arrive at a balanced life.

There have been very few people like Socrates or Plato who really were able, by philosophical thought and contemplation of values, to get very excited about virtue. But there are many people, who are not even Christians, who make a commendable attempt at it. But abstractions have very little power. This is the mistake that not only Plato and Socrates, but all philosophers, have made. Reason, appealing though it may be, suffers from an anemia. It really doesn't have the power to help us regulate the passions.

Another approach to the problem is the ascetic approach, or the legalistic approach: we deny ourselves as many passions as possible, even deny ourselves exposure to them. The idea is to master our thoughts. Some ancients held that one should never live in a house, or the desire for a nice house would overwhelm his better judgment. Others said that one should never eat steak, or he would begin to aspire to all kinds of inordinate appetites. They suggested that if you would use a little cracked wheat and water, and never tasted how good steak was, you would be satisfied. By diminishing your appreciation of things your life would be safely hemmed in.

Even within the Christian tradition, which is a stranger to this form of thinking, we have the rise of legalism and monasticism. This philosophy of life said, "Get away from life, deny yourself satisfaction, and live as simply as possible so that you will not be tempted." But trying to reduce our desires can lead to corruption. The medieval monasteries were often worse centers of depravity and degeneracy than the population at large, although this is by no means universally true.

The Christian message and the Christian concern with the regulation of the passions does not rely on developing a love for abstractions of philosophy, nor does it rely on the path of asceticism and denial in the classical sense. But it relies, in the words of Thomas Chalmers, on "the expulsive power of a new affection."[1] the development of a master passion in life which is so strong that it can regulate all the lesser passions and put them in order. The key to understanding this is the wisdom expounded in the Bible.

You will recall the discussion of how wisdom becomes a person in Proverbs. Wisdom is not an abstraction; wisdom is a being. In the New Testament Paul calls Jesus Christ the wisdom of God (see 1 Cor. 1:30). John calls Christ *logos* (see John 1:1), which can mean reason and is closely related to the Hebrew word *chokmah* for wisdom.

Jesus Christ is the wisdom and the power of God. Jesus Christ is wisdom: not an abstraction, but the Person who enters and changes our lives. As the wisdom of God, He not only tells us how we should govern our passions, but is in fact the power through which we may govern them.

Let me go back to Greek mythology, to the era of the Argonauts. Odysseus is sailing with his crew on a series of dangerous adventures. One adventure takes them past the island inhabited by the sirens. Now these creatures have the bodies of birds, the heads of women, and very beautiful voices. When the sirens begin to sing, passing sailors are so entranced that they rush toward the island in order to encounter these lovely creatures, only to be smashed to pieces and destroyed on the dangerous rocks and the treacherous surf around the island. This story is where we get the expression, "the siren voice of pleasure." The hunger for pleasure is so great that we ignore the perils; yet in reaching our desire we find ourselves shipwrecked. (The siren myth is very much like the Teutonic myth of the Lorelei.)

Now Odysseus didn't know how he was going to get by. There were two ways it could be done. First, by equipment. Odysseus plugged up all of the sailors' ears and had them lash him to a mast so he couldn't move.

But somebody came up with a better idea. There was on board the ship a man who was the greatest harp player of them all, Orpheus. (Have you ever heard of the Orpheum Theatre? That comes from the Greeks too.) Orpheus made the most beautiful music on his harp—far more beautiful than the singing of the sirens. Thus as the men listened to the music of Orpheus they were not tempted by the songs of the sirens.

Do I need to interpret the ancient myth? What we need in our lives is a passion for something that transcends all of our other passions. Then we will hear the voice of God and be unmoved by the siren voices of unregulated passion which would lead us to destruction. Then we can satisfy many of those legitimate appetites in their proper order. We need to create a relationship with God that is so strong that it can dominate any other passion of life. This is the road to mastery.

Is this not the very story of Joseph? One of the patriarchs of Israel, he was once the overseer for

Potiphar, captain of the guards in the land of Egypt. When Potiphar's wife tried to seduce him he fled from the house crying, "How shall I sin against my God?" (See Gen. 39.) There was an affection for God so strong that it could drown any natural passion. This is the wisdom of God. It is Christ, the power of God, who by His grace can create that kind of passion in our lives.

Teach us this day, our Father, that there is no other way to avoid shipwreck in life than to come to grips with the necessity of deferred satisfaction. That while the road of philosophical contemplation is a noble and meaningful way of regulating our passions, it is ultimately too weak and powerless. That while self-denial and asceticism may be a well meant attempt to regulate our passions, it is ultimately a failure. We thank You for Jesus Christ, the wisdom and the power of God, who alone is able to create within us such a love for Himself and to pour upon our lives such grace that we all may achieve mastery in life. May each of us who know Him so purify our hearts in confession that we may sense the power of His loving presence. May this unseen presence so attract strangers that, by opening their lives in simple surrender, they may perceive the reality of Jesus Christ, the wisdom and power of God. Amen.

footnote

1. Andrew Blackwood, ed., *The Protestant Pulpit*
(New York: Abingdon Press, 1974), pp. 50–62.

Young man, obey your father and your mother. Tie their instructions around your finger so you won't forget. Take to heart all of their advice. Every day and all night long their counsel will lead you and save you from harm; when you wake up in the morning, let their instruction guide you into the new day. For their advice is a beam of light directed into the dark corners of your mind to warn you of danger and to give you a good life. Proverbs 6:20–23, *TLB*

WISDOM
AND
FILIAL
PIETY

Wisdom, as explored in Proverbs, involves many practical areas of human life. Here in Proverbs 6 we see the wisdom of filial piety, which is the proper regard for both the person and the opinions of our parents.

Before exploring the positive aspects of filial piety, I want to point to some of its perils. The great hymn, "Faith of Our Fathers," celebrates not only faith in God but the mood of filial piety.

"Faith of our fathers! living still
In spite of dungeon, fire, and sword:
How sweet would be their children's fate,
If they, like them, could die for Thee!"

It's a picture of the deep relationship between regard for parents and regard for the faith which they have given us. You will catch the irony of this if you realize the context in which the hymn was written. It was written over one hundred and twenty years ago, not by a Protestant, but by a Roman Catholic in an Ulster jail in Ireland. There was a Protestant mob outside trying to break down the doors to lynch him. It was a very contemporary hymn.

We usually imagine it to be a Protestant hymn coming out of the period of the Reformation when the Protestants were in prison about to be lynched by Catholic mobs. But it was a Catholic about to be lynched by a Protestant mob.

It is sweet to have a faith you could die for. But as C. S. Lewis has pointed out, those who are willing to die for their faith easily become willing to kill for it.[1] That is the tragedy of Ulster, and of all the other religious wars with their intolerance and bitterness and hatred.

When we attempt to understand what the Bible has to say about filial piety, we should be careful to understand it in the biblical sense and not in a sense of uncritical adoration of parents and blind submission to whatever they happen to believe.

There is a feeling today that submission to parents is part of an authoritarian age which has passed away. And certainly the most conservative of us have no desire to return to the ancient Germanic or Teutonic concept of "Herr Father", or worse, to the "father" concept of ancient Rome. In ancient Rome the father had a right, without incurring any legal penalties whatsoever, to kill his children if they displeased him. The right of life and death over the children was held by father. This was not a Christian concept.

Even in this century we have seen elements of excessive authoritarianism. Germany's Hitler, Japan's Tojo and China's Mao are embodiments of it. Such patriarchal authoritarianism must never be confused with filial piety.

But let us not undermine the biblical teaching with unbiblical reactions. A reaction to excessive authoritarianism is found in the current left-wing attack upon the family. Even so renowned a sociologist and anthropologist as Margaret Mead tells us in *Culture & Commitment* that we must totally reorganize our society because children today know more than their parents do. Their education is much better and knowledge is changing so rapidly, says Mead, that it is ridiculous for parents to assume that they have the right to tell their children what to do.[2]

An even more extreme attack on the family appears in a book by David Cooper.[3] This man is a Marxist; he believes that the family is responsible for all the tragedies of our modern world. It is the upper class's attempt to manipulate children into submissiveness so they will not instigate revolution or demand justice and equality.

Cooper suggests that the emotionally disturbed children, those who simply cannot submit to authority—literally the insane children—are the people we ought to encourage to bring down the entire social structure and set up a classless society. Enforcing conformity upon the developing personality of the child stifles his autonomy and denies him selfhood, according to Cooper. In that setting, he says, mental illness is a more appropriate response than tame capitulation. So he urges joining the disturbed kids and helping them tear down society.

The family is evil, says Cooper, and will be replaced by a sort of democratic "communalism" which will

61

usher in a great era of peace and joy. I doubt that anybody reading this book really believes that. I don't think Mr. Cooper believes it himself, but he gets plenty of publicity by making such outlandish claims.

It is interesting that the Bible itself does not subscribe to a totally authoritarian picture of the family relationship. Look at the Person of our Lord Jesus Christ. He goes to the Temple at twelve years of age and apparently forgets about His parents. They leave for home, then they miss Him and start searching. When His mother finally finds Him in the Temple disputing with the scholars, she scolds Him, and He replies, "I must be about My Father's business, you know." (See Luke 2:41–52.) It hardly sounds like total abject submission to the wishes of the parents.

In His adult ministry, Jesus often attacked the elders of Israel. Remember, the concept of elders in a society is very closely related to the idea of veneration of parents. In Matthew 7 much of that great Sermon on the Mount is an attack on the traditions of the elders who had made the Word of God of no effect. Christ attacked the patriarchal structure of Israel.

The apostle Paul could, in one sense, never have sung, "Faith of our Fathers living still. . . ." He left the faith of his father. He repudiated it in one sense, though we have to qualify that statement very carefully. But he was not a man who submitted to a belief just because his parents believed it.

The great leaders of the church, Luther and Calvin, had the courage to examine the faith which their parents practiced, and to say, "It is wrong and I reject it."

When we lead young people in the community to Christ, and their parents are not Christians, we are, in a sense, undermining the authority of those homes. We do so in the name of the Word of God. We must then qualify our understandings of filial piety with the above considerations.

With these cautions in mind, let's move on to examine the power of filial piety. The Bible is filled with it. Not only in Proverbs, but many passages teach the importance of it.

One of the great commandments is: "Honor your father and your mother, that your days may be prolonged in the land which the Lord your God gives you" (Exod. 20:12, *NASB*). Paul echoes it in Ephesians: "Children, obey your parents in the Lord, for this is right. Honor your father and mother (which is the first commandment with a promise) . . ." (Eph. 6:1,2 *NASB*).

Sometimes, in order to obey God, we may have to go against our parents' wishes. But there is no time when we may dishonor them. In the case of unworthy parents, there is the honor due them as persons, as those who have sacrificed something for us even though we have suffered wrong at their hands.

The apostle Paul, it is true, repudiated the Jewish orthodoxy of his parents for the new Christian religion. But in defending himself before Felix, he said, "I do serve the God of our fathers, believing everything that is in accordance with the Law, and that is written in the Prophets" (Acts 24:14, *NASB*).

His conversion was not totally a repudiation, but rather a fulfillment. "I'm really going back to the true religion of the fathers," he says.

63

Jesus Christ, when He spoke of the traditions of the elders, said, "Think not that I am come to destroy the law, or the prophets: I am not come to destroy, but to fulfill. . . . One jot or one tittle shall in no wise pass from the law, till all be fulfilled" (Matt. 5:17,18). Jesus was not an anarchistic revolutionary, nor a man who believed in overthrowing the standards of the ages. He was indeed far more rigorous morally than even the Pharisees whom He attacked.

And while certainly some of the sayings of Jesus to His own mother seem strong to our ears, let us remember that He never ceased to honor her. In the hour of His most intense suffering, His attention was not on His own needs, but on the welfare of His mother. He pointed to John the beloved disciple and said, "Behold thy mother!" and He said to His mother, "Woman, behold thy son!" (John 19:27,26). An adoption ceremony was completed right there, in the extremity of His own agony. Whatever question we may have about the attitude of Jesus toward His mother, we see that in the most intensely crucial hour of His life His regard was more for her and her welfare than His own.

May I suggest also that many of the secular attacks on the family are without justification. The Marxist attack on the family really isn't a very good one. The Russians tried to abolish the family, but it didn't work. The critics of Mr. Cooper (who wants to abolish the family) point out that there is nothing more unstable and more imminently capable of total collapse than the very communes that he's advocating to replace the family. His only answer seems to be, "Well, naturally that's due to the capitalist corruption that's around. But once the glorious revolution comes there won't be any of that and the commune will be stable." Which proposition, since it has never been demonstrated, requires a defiant leap of faith against all reason and experience. With such pure romanticism, Marxism again shows its unbounded enthusiasm for fantasy.

When Winston Churchill was listening to the criticism of democracy, he said, "It's the worst of all possible governments until one begins to consider the next alternative." We might paraphrase him by saying that the family is the worst possible arrangement until you consider the alternative. Then it becomes a vital necessity for the nurture of all life.

Underlying so much of the talk we hear today is the idea that because we are young, we know more, and only the young achieve things. And it is certainly true that many great things have been accomplished by young people both today and yesterday. But let me remind you that Moses was an octogenarian, over eighty years of age, when he led the children of Israel out of Egypt. Let me remind you that Winston Churchill was of retirement age when he came to save Britain from the onslaughts of the Nazis in the Second World War. David Ben-Gurion was in his sixties when he read the "Proclamation on the Rise of the State of Israel," thus declaring the existence and independence of that state; he then became its first prime minister and brought it through its first trying years of nationhood. Remember it was Conrad Adenauer, a septuagenarian and ultimately an octogenarian, who rebuilt Germany after the Second World War—a task far more significant than all the machinations of Adolf Hitler. Remember it was Charles De-Gaulle—a man way up in his seventies who could neither see nor hear well—who salvaged France from the brink of revolution and led his country to relative stability while in office as president.

I am citing too many conservatives. Remember that both Chou and Mao are in their late seventies, and the guiding light of the New Left is not some bright young man of twenty-five, but the aging Herbert Marcuse in his seventies.

I think this business of old and young has got to go. What we have are remarkable people. If they're remarkable when they are young they need to be given leadership, and they should be allowed to keep that leadership when they are old. We need to stand up against a society that says, "You're not worth listening to because you're a teen-ager," or, "Drop dead, you're over the hill, old man." We need to start listening to people who, by virtue of their wisdom at any age, have something to tell us. Take parents, for example: they do teach us to walk, to talk. The very fact that they have survived as parents, and survived as husband and wife, and survived emotionally and economically in our time—just that simple fact alone is worthy of some respect.

Let me conclude by pointing to what I hope will be the path of filial piety for all of us. First of all, let me speak to the young. That includes all who have parents living, no matter how old you are. Honor your father and your mother. Remember, respect is due every human being. And your incapacity to accept this fact in regard to your parents, who have a very significant relationship with you, will destroy

66

your capacity to relate to anybody else. Don't think you can have a lousy relationship with your parents and have a good relationship with everyone else. That simply doesn't work. It's empirically demonstrable in terms of psychological studies, and it's obvious common sense. Even the worst parent is worthy of respect as a person.

One of the steps toward psychological maturity is the capacity to accept responsibility for our own attitude. Regardless of how wrong our parents have been, we have to assume responsibility for our own anger, bitterness and hostility. Otherwise, there's no way out. Psychologists tell us that ultimately we have to say, "I realize there has been injustice, but I have allowed bitterness and anger to grow in my life. I have to take responsibility and cope with these feelings; until I do that, there will be no possibility for emotional or spiritual wholeness." This is true according to the Bible. If you still cannot accept the sinfulness of your parents and give them love and respect, I think you will discover that you will also be unable to accept your own sinfulness and give yourself the proper respect. Get hung up in your relationships with your parents and you'll never get in a right relationship with yourself.

The biblical standard of honoring and obeying parents does not mean that children are without recourse. The church does not endorse carte blanche everything that parents do or say. We are not under Roman law. The civil law reflects the Christian understanding of the relationship between human beings. The laws of the land say parents are denied the right to do certain things to their children. Young people in our church have recourse with us if their parents have moved beyond rationality and reason in their relationship. Neither I, as a pastor, nor the elders of a church, will hesitate to use discipline on parents if they transgress what is reasonably expected of parents and children. I have done this. My deacons in former churches have done this. Parents are a part of the family, and they are under the authority of the church. The church will use its discipline under God in unreasonable and extreme situations.

But I want you to remember, above all, Jesus Christ, because "He learned obedience from the things which He suffered" (Heb. 5:8, *NASB*). Do you know what His Father asked Him to do? His Father asked Him to die. And He said, "Father, save Me from this hour." There wasn't any voice, but He knew there was an answer, and He said, "Okay. I guess this is why I came. Not My will but Yours be done." (See Luke 22:42.)

We parents need to be careful how we use our authority. The same Bible that says, "Children, obey your parents" (Eph. 6:1), says also "Provoke not your children to wrath" (Eph. 6:4). This is like the passages on marriage. "Wives, obey your husbands; husbands, love your wives." Most often these are clubs with which we hit each other. Father says, "The Bible says, 'Children, obey your parents' "; and kid says, "But the Bible says, 'Provoke not your children to wrath!' " That is not how the Bible was intended to be used. Instead, I should ask, "Am I really being a parent or am I just getting rid of some frustrations?"

I realized recently what a really frightful figure I can be to my little girls. I'm not only three times their size, but the "Larsenian" bellow can be terrifying. It is easy to overwhelm their little personalities with terror. Maybe one of the reasons children are unable to give due respect to parents is that parents have not shown due regard for the personhood of their children. They have overwhelmed children by the sheer power of their large bodies and their more developed minds and lungs.

I remember having to discipline my older daughter by spanking her. When the deed was done, she said, "I am going to my room and close the door," and in she went and slammed the door.

I said to my wife, "She's not going to get away with that."

And she said to me, "Now just a minute. You humiliated our little three-year-old. And she had to be punished because she was wrong. But you've got to give her some right to feel bad."

One of my dearest friends has seven children who have all turned out to be fine Christians. The funny thing is, he's a temperamental, authoritarian type. He blows his lid easily and jumps to conclusions too quickly, but the kids love him. First of all, he plays with them; and second, while he never tolerates defiance, they can always take him into the back room after it's all over and say, "You were unjust and unfair with me."

I think one of our problems is that we experience a lot of frustration and anger in life. Then our children get out of line, and because they are weak, and we have moral justification, we vent more anger than the occasion demands. We wouldn't dare speak to our boss because we might lose our job. We wouldn't speak to our wife because she would go home to mother, but we dare speak to our children for whom we would really like to give our whole lives. I'm reminded of those famous words, "We only hurt the people we love."

The psalmist said, "He (God) has not dealt with us according to our sins, nor rewarded us according to our iniquities" (Psalm 103:10, *NASB*). If you really understand a right relationship with God, you will rightly relate to both your parents and your children.

Father, teach us how to be both good parents and children. Give us a proper regard for the personhood of everyone, especially our children and our parents. And give us a clear vision of our relationship to You, our Father. Through Jesus Christ our Lord. Amen.

footnotes

1. C. S. Lewis, *Reflections on the Psalms* (New York: Harcourt and Brace Co., 1958), p. 28.
2. Margaret Mead, *Culture and Commitment* (New York: Doubleday and Co., Inc., 1970), pp. 66–101.
3. David Cooper, *Death of the Family* (New York: Random House, Inc., 1970), p. 145.

My words are plain and clear to
anyone with half a mind—if it is only
open!   Proverbs 8:9, *TLB*

7

WISDOM
AND
CLEVERNESS

Wisdom. The simplicity of integrity is the profundity of wisdom. As we continue our studies in the nature of wisdom, this proposition must surely be nailed down as one of the fundamental perceptions of the Hebrew Christian concept of wisdom. Integrity is the moral dimension that separates wisdom from intelligence, learning and cleverness.

The first proposition that I should like to suggest is that wisdom is not cleverness, although it seems very closely related to matters such as knowledge, intelligence and learning. We can see wisdom is sometimes applied even to the rather simple world of nature. For instance, we realize that an ant would probably flunk a Stanford-Binet IQ test. It wouldn't even register on the imbecile scale. Yet ants seem capable of organizing themselves in communities and storing up food for the winter, although they have never experienced a winter before. That's why we can say to the lazy man, "Go to the ant, O sluggard, observe her ways and be wise" (Prov. 6:6, *NASB*). She seems to have a perception of the future. She is able to make plans, so to speak.

Or watch an oriole make a nest. An oriole not a year old, skilled and capable of making a little cradle in which to deposit the eggs which will soon be hatching into new little birds. And we say nature has wisdom.

Even in the simplicity, the want of learning, in the animal world we see a form of wisdom. And modern man, despite his tremendous amassment of knowledge, seems at times to be afflicted with an unimaginable stupidity. The men who planned the wars that have scarred the face of the earth were not unintelligent. The art of warfare and the art of politics are two of the most studied and developed of the disciplines of mankind. Yet despite the available knowledge, these disciplines are afflicted with profound stupidity and folly. For they leave us on the brink of holocaust and human suffering. What man, what woman on the face of the earth, would look you in the eye and say, "I want war. I want violence and bloodshed to touch me"?

Even those with professional knowledge sometimes lack wisdom. The marriage counselor enters divorce court, in spite of all his credentials, to divorce his own wife. The psychiatrist commits suicide. The clergyman leaves his profession and runs off with some young woman, despite his many years of preparation and experience. The economist goes bankrupt as he plays the stock market.

74

There is a folly to human understanding. There is an ignorance to human learning. There is an incompetence which we must admit to all of man's science, even without taking away one centimeter of gratitude and appreciation for all that human learning has brought to us.

We must make a distinction between wisdom and learning. Or perhaps we can do as Paul does—distinguish between two kinds of learning, or two kinds of wisdom. He speaks of "the wisdom of this world" (1 Cor. 1:20), the wisdom that does not know God. And he speaks of the wisdom that knows God, which may seem foolish because it is something that even the most simple can appropriate. The message of Jesus Christ, in terms of human philosophical systems, does not appeal to man's intellect.

Paul says, "I know very well how foolish it sounds to those who are lost, when they hear that Jesus died to save them. But we who are saved recognize this message as the very power of God. For God says, 'I will destroy all human plans of salvation no matter how wise they seem to be, and ignore the best ideas of men, even the most brilliant of them.'

"So what about these wise men, these scholars, these brilliant debaters of this world's great affairs? God has made them all look foolish, and shown their wisdom to be useless nonsense. For God in his wisdom saw to it that the world would never find God through human brilliance, and then he stepped in and saved all those who believed his message, which the world calls foolish and silly. It seems foolish to the Jews because they want a sign from heaven as proof that what is preached is true; and it is foolish to the Gentiles because they believe only what agrees with their philosophy and seems wise to them.

"So when we preach about Christ dying to save them, the Jews are offended and the Gentiles say it's all nonsense. But God has opened the eyes of those called to salvation, both Jews and Gentiles, to see that Christ is the mighty power of God to save them; Christ himself is the center of God's wise plan for their salvation. This so-called 'foolish' plan of God is far wiser than the wisest plan of the wisest man, and God in his weakness—Christ dying on the cross—is far stronger than any man" (1 Cor. 1:18–25, *TLB*).

This is the paradox of wisdom. It is never to be confused with brilliance, intelligence, learning or cleverness. It is a higher wisdom, which wise men in their folly have deemed foolish. But I started at the outset by saying that the simplicity of integrity is the profundity of wisdom. It is not necessarily antagonistic to all human wisdom, understanding and brilliance. But without a moral dimension which is available to even the most simple and unlearned, all human knowledge becomes folly.

Wisdom is integrity. It is wise to perceive that the fundamental basis of life is relational. That's why the writer of the Proverbs makes wisdom into a person. Wisdom recognizes that the ultimate center of the human universe is personal. And the only adequate relationship between persons is the relationship of love, love for God, love for each other, love for our enemies. That is the heart of all relationships, the heart of the universe.

Love cannot be perceived through the sciences. It

is a spiritual and moral perception. And the only relationship that love can sustain is the relationship of integrity. If there is integrity of relationships between people there is wisdom.

Even a scientist cannot get along without integrity. He has to trust that the scientific data he obtains from others is reliable. Even sciences are based on this prior commitment to honor and truthfulness.

"Listen to me! For I have important information for you. Everything I say is right and true, for I hate lies and every kind of deception.... If anyone respects and fears God, he will hate evil. For wisdom hates pride, arrogance, corruption and deceit of every kind" (Prov. 8:6,7,13, *TLB*).

Phoniness and deception are the very evidence of the breakdown of love, the only vital force in the universe. And unless we perceive that relationship is at the heart of the universe and that love is the basis of all relationships and that falsehood is the rupture of all love, we have not come to understand the meaning of the divine wisdom. Trustworthiness, candor and integrity are the qualities without which all learning becomes diabolical and evil.

This is expressed rather well in a letter that the famous prince of preachers, Charles Spurgeon, wrote to the prime minister of Great Britain, William Gladstone. Gladstone himself was a devout Christian and certainly one of the great statesmen of the nineteenth century. Spurgeon wrote to him in the following fashion. "You do not know how those of us regard you who feel it a joy to live when a premier believes in righteousness. We believe in no man's infallibility, but it is restful to be sure of one man's integrity."[1]

I suppose this is what makes so many of us suspicious of politicians, even though politics can be a most noble art. We are suspicious not that the man might make a mistake, but that staying in office is more important to him than honor and candor. We suspect his integrity.

Wisdom is not cleverness, it is integrity. Thus wisdom can belong to the simple. Notice this. "O foolish ones, let me show you common sense! . . . My words are plain and clear to anyone with half a mind—if it is only open!" (Prov. 8:5,9, *TLB*). God's kingdom is equalitarian. As we saw in Paul's famous passage in 1 Corinthians, God in His wisdom determined that He could not be found by human brilliance, otherwise salvation would be a function of the intelligence quotient. Only the smart people would be saved. And that would leave most of us in a rather tragic position.

But salvation is something that even the most simple can grasp. It is not too simple for the profoundly educated intellectual of our time, yet it is simple enough for the smallest child to grasp. Notice the words of our Lord Jesus as recorded in the Gospel of Luke: "Then he was filled with the joy of the Holy Spirit and said, 'I praise you, O Father, Lord of heaven and earth, for hiding these things from the intellectuals and worldly wise and for revealing them to those who are as trusting as little children'" (Luke 10:21, *TLB*).

It is interesting to see that Jesus makes it a faith for children. I suppose this is why so many people have felt that Christianity is childish. But that betrays a failure to understand the vast distinction between childlike and childish. As children we display a spontaneity of profound integrity and wisdom, but unfortunately maturation soon takes these traits from us.

Jesus was not the only one who saw that children have built-in wisdom. Professor Edward Carnell, in reflecting on the contributions of the great psychoanalyst Sigmund Freud, observed that the conclusion of Freud and the conclusion of Jesus were not all that far apart. He says, "Freud taught his patients the art of seeing themselves through their own childhood. He believed that people became anxious and thus lessen their chances of leading happy, normal lives, because somewhere . . . they have lost the natural zest and unconditional faith of childhood."[2] In the process of psychoanalysis the client undergoes what is called regression. He goes back to early forms of childhood behavior and tends to put his life back together again, to grow up right rather than twisted and deformed.

There is something about children, a spontaneous perception of goodness which we sometimes miss. Since what children really want is love and affection, they can be solaced without all kinds of cunning manipulations. They don't really understand what deception is all about, at least until they're a year or two old. They can't understand it when they encounter it in people. They do not know how to manipulate in the conscious sense of that word. They don't have problems with understanding right from wrong. We adults say right and wrong is a matter of opinion. We're sure that nobody knows what right and wrong is. But you tell a child the story of Cinderella and her stepmother and ask who is the good one and who is the bad one, and you'll find out.

They know. You never find a child who'll tell you that the wicked stepmother was the good one, and that Cinderella, who was polite and kind to everyone, was the bad one. Children see that these are the fundamental qualities of life; they have a blind faith that in the end those who are kind and truthful will come out all right. Now, you see, we're adults and we're not so sure about any of this.

In our confused world today every evil is praised as a virtue and every virtue is damned as a vice. But the child will still tell you that Cinderella was good and the stepmother was bad, because one was kind and truthful and the other was mean and selfish.

Our problem is that we complicate things through pride. When we soon see that love has to suffer because it is vulnerable to being hurt, we learn the art of untruthfulness and concealment. We learn to make impressions which are not genuine. Carnell tells us, "Pride draws us away from the kingdom of love . . . by tempting us to think that we can dispense with the duties of love."[3] Pride says that a person is good when he is powerful not when he is kind and truthful. This sort of pride is the cynicism of modern "wisdom."

We see the final conclusion of Paul: "The world by wisdom knew not God" (1 Cor. 1:21). Or hear the words of our Saviour: "Blessed are the pure in heart: for they shall see God" (Matt. 5:8). The modern movement which proclaims the death of God is nothing more than the death of man's moral conscience, the blindness wrought by the loss of his integrity.

The first step to becoming wise is to admit that we are foolish. Humility is the path of wisdom. A child has no trouble admitting that it needs its mother. It doesn't have any shame in admitting that it is helpless and in need of strength. But we have created the myths of our self-sufficiency and our autonomy. Some people boast that they don't even need God.

We need to be honest in our frailty. Jesus said, "Except ye be converted, and become as little children, ye shall not enter into the kingdom of heaven" (Matt. 18:3). When we become honest with ourselves about our own frailty we shall begin to recover our moral perceptions about truth and integrity. Then we shall know the difference between true prophets and false prophets, between true religion and false religion, between right and wrong. We shall encounter the wisdom of God, and if He has never crossed our awareness before, Jesus of Nazareth will cross our mind, and with the eyes of integrity we shall perceive in Him the wisdom and the power of God. To study, to look at and to observe Jesus of Nazareth with the eyes of integrity, is to be persuaded by His very Person and to be won to His Lordship.

Here is a short piece which I have found handwritten in my file. I do not know where it came from. Let it draw the Person of Jesus across your conscience, that in the integrity of your humility you may perceive in Him the wisdom of God, and surrender to His Lordship—Jesus the Son of God, Redeemer of Israel, Lion of the tribe of Judah, Lord of lords and King of kings.

"There may be another Homer, there may be another Virgil, there may be another Dante, there may be another Milton, but there will never be another Jesus. Whatever surprises there may be in store for the world, Jesus will never be surpassed. He is the goal of all goodness, the summit of all thought, the crown of all character and the perfection of all beauty. He is the incarnation of all tenderness, the focalization of force, the manifestation of might, the personification of power, the concentration of character, the materialization of thought, and the living illustration of all truth. He is the prophecy of man's possibility.

"We behold Him, and in Him we see the realization of all human expectation: a leader greater than Moses, a priest greater than Aaron, a king greater than David, a commander greater than Joshua, a philosopher greater than Solomon and a prophet greater than Elijah. He walks like a man. He talks like God. His words are oracles, His acts miracles. The crown of divinity rests on His brow. The sceptre of universal dominion clings to His hand, the eternities flash in His eyes. Eternal rectitude is written in His face; the smile of Jehovah transforms His countenance.

"He is the express image of His father. Children cluster at his feet. Womanhood instinctively places the crown of purity on His brow. The winds obey Him. A glance from His eye and the crystal waters blush to amber wine. The dead forget themselves and live. The lame leap for joy. Ears which never heard thirst for the very sound of His voice and sightless eyes deny their past and open their drooping lids to the beauty of His presence. Pain, palsied at His touch, vanishes.

"The name of Jesus stands alone. God has given Him a name which is above every name. No creed can contain Him, no catechism can expound Him, flesh of our flesh, very God of our very God. To be a Christian is to live in Christ. Unto Him be glory, dominion and power for ever and ever. Amen." (Source Unknown.)

Teach us, O God, that the simplicity of integrity is the profundity of wisdom. And grant, our Father, that the road to that integrity is the road of becoming honest and open as a child. Given that humble perception, give us the grace to behold the Person of Jesus Christ who is the wisdom and the power of God. Amen.

footnotes

1. John M. Morley, *Life of William Ewart Gladstone,* vol. II (New York: The Macmillan Co., 1903), p. 531

2. Edward Carnell, *The Kingdom of Love and the Pride of Life* (Grand Rapids: Wm B. Eerdmans Publishing Co., 1960), pp. 6,7.

3. Carnell, *Kingdom of Love,* p. 22.

For the reverence and fear of God are basic to all wisdom. Knowing God results in every other kind of understanding. Proverbs 9:10, *TLB*

WISDOM
AND
KNOWING
GOD

As we study <u>Proverbs 9:10</u>, let us begin with its second sentence: "<u>Knowing God results in every other kind of understanding.</u>" I suppose when we think of every other kind of understanding, we think of scientific knowledge, ethical knowledge and self-knowledge. The problem with this is that, at least at first blush, it's false. Being devout does not make one a great scientist. I don't know about you, but when I have to have an appendectomy I'd rather have a Moslem surgeon than a Christian plumber!

But the statement is historically true, nonetheless, even though it is not immediately true in every man's experience. The rise of modern science and technology is a result of the Christian understanding of the universe and God. You can see this in the first chapter of Francis Schaeffer's book, *The Church at the End of the Twentieth Century,* where he reviews the philosophical foundations of modern science, as we find in Galileo and Newton and others. Modern philosophers who do not have a Christian reference admit this completely. Alfred North Whitehead, the famous philosopher, and even the great scientist, J. R. Oppenheimer, tell us that the foundations of modern science are based upon the Christian assumption that the universe is rational because God is its Creator. Because the universe is rational and man is created in the image of God, man also is rational; and thus he is able to understand what makes the world go round. Out of this fundamental commitment to the rationality of the universe and the rationality of man have come the assumptions and the experiments that have brought to life all modern science and technology. This fundamental assumption was the impetus that gave rise to modern learning.

Now modern man has repudiated the idea that the universe is created and directed by a rational God. Cutting off these roots (our assumption that God created the universe), leads to a "cut-flower civilization." We find that modern science begins to lose its faith that the universe can be rationally understood. There is a very interesting movement developing known as "the cult of madness." This movement holds that the way to find out the essence of life is not through rational procedures but through insanity and madness, what Nietzsche calls the "Dionysian spirit."[1]

We're also discovering that a man is credited not because he is scientific but because he subscribes to certain contemporary orthodoxies. I know of a famous physicist who has some rather unpopular views with regard to race (and I pray they are wrong). He's about to lose his professional standing as a physicist because he entertains an unpopular social view. Irrationality has now come to birth in our society, even in the lives of scientists, because they have cut off their convictions about God. Rephrasing the wise man's statement we can safely say that not knowing God results in every other kind of scientific misunderstanding.

Not only in the scientific realm but also in the ethical realm, there are many good people who do not believe in God. We see noble and honest things done by people who have rejected the Christian or even the theistic understanding of the universe. But this, too, is cut-flower morality. It soon fades. Nothing can sustain it, because it leads to questions like, "Why ought one to be good?" or "What is good?" Hence the tremendous moral confusion of our time.

Will Herberg, one of the great analysts of our culture, says people don't believe in standards anymore. There is hardly a virtue that is not damned as a vice, and hardly a vice that is not praised as a virtue. People think that modern psychology can provide an ethical foundation. It can't.

Unless you have a universe that is moral at the heart, unless you have a God who commands, you create moral chaos. Unfortunately this has reached all levels today. It has even reached into the church. Some churches now are in the process of ordaining sexual deviates! And the interesting thing is that even in the arguments about whether such practices are right or wrong, nobody asks, "What does God say about this?" No wonder the churches are empty. The wise man was right: Only by knowing God can there be every kind of ethical understanding.

And surely it is true that knowing God results in every kind of self-understanding. The big crisis of our time, we say, is the sense of alienation and the loss of identity. This is the cry of the secular psychologist, anthropologist and sociologist and all the other kinds of 'ologists. Why? Because if you look at the external world without God, what identity has a man? You're just a remarkable conglomeration of protoplasm. In the long span of history you are nothing. In the dimensions of the universe you are a speck of dust, scarcely of any more significance than the roach you squashed on the sidewalk this morning. You have no meaning, you have no identity, you have no self-worth. You are nothing.

If we look at what man has done to this universe, he is little more than a disease; he's a scum, an eczema about to poison himself in the filth of his own living.

But when you believe that man was created by God in His image, you know that man is of infinite value, so loved by the Author of the universe that He sent His only Son to die. Then you are something! Unless you begin with the premise of God, you will end up believing that you are nothing.

There's an old parable about a spider. He decided one day to move, so he spun a long strand of web up in the barn rafter, and he lowered himself to the next level. He fastened himself to a two-by-four and began to spin a great web. By and by he died and went to the great beyond, or wherever it is that spiders go. And of course, he left his estate to his son, who in turn left it to his own son. But the carefully built structure was a little antique at that point and as the grandson was marching along one day, he tripped over a strand of spider web. So he said, "These are out of style right now and they are in the way. I think the first step of remodeling will be to cut this strand." So he reached out and nipped off what just happened to be the strand upon which the whole web was hanging, and he fell instantly to his death on the barn floor below.

What's the point of that silly story? This is what modern man is doing to his life. The fact of God as the foundation of life is the strand upon which all life and understanding rests. But modern man has decided that God is an antique which, in the remodeling of our life-style, may be abandoned and dispensed with. That is why we are now beginning to get the sickening feeling that our whole society is going to collapse. And if I may take liberty with words, this is why Reich's "Greening of America" will not save America. Rather, that greening is gangrene, an ominous symptom of the fact that we are dying. For the writer of the Proverbs was correct when he said, "Knowing God results in every other kind of understanding."

And this leads me to the second half of my study. *Not only is the knowledge of God the foundation of every other kind of understanding, but "the fear of the Lord is the beginning of wisdom."* Now most of us moderns are convinced that a religion of fear is bad religion, that you should not generally scare people into being good. A religion based on fear ultimately becomes a destructive and frightening thing in terms of the consequences it produces. The only value that religion has for most moderns is that it takes away our fears; so it's hardly a good introduction for a faith to suggest that the way to get rid of our fears is to become afraid.

But let's look a little more deeply at this dilemma. The greatest peril in coming to any kind of knowledge is to confuse wishing with knowing. There is quite a difference. To wish something to be true is not the same as knowing it to be true. Most of us would like to make a killing in the stock market with our few dollars. We'd like to find the kind of stock that pays out a hundred-to-one. But the worst kind of investor you can be is one who has confused wishing with knowing. And the wise investor is the man who knows how to be afraid. His fears purify his wishes.

Wishing there was peace does not open the road to peace. That is the road for knowledge and wisdom to pursue.

The trouble with most people is that their religion is not based on knowledge, it is based upon wishing. They believe not in the God who is there, but in the God whom they would like to be there. The enemies of religion have observed this with telling astuteness. It was Ludwig Feuerbach, the German atheist-philosopher two generations back, who said sarcastically, "Christians have always believed that God creates man in his own image; that is not correct. The truth is, that man creates God in his own image." He was wrong in the first sentence, but what he said in the second sentence is all too often correct. We have created the God we wish to exist.

I hear so often in modern theology that we cannot accept the God that the Bible tells us about. Since man cannot believe in Him, what kind of a God can he believe in? And then we proceed to build a theology about our created God. But creating a theology doesn't bring God into existence. That is known as wishful thinking. The whole foundation of modern liberal theology is based on the premise that modern man has to change his conceptions of God in order to believe. The heart of this belief is a fundamental error and fallacy of the most tragic, tragic sort.

And it creeps over into fine orthodox circles. People say, "Well, you know, I don't believe in a God who is full of anger and judgment as in the Old Testament. I believe in a God who is loving and sweet and kind." You've heard that. How much of that is based on what God has revealed Himself to be, and how much on that which you wish He were? Someone says, "I don't believe in a religion of fear." Is that because a religion of fear is a false religion, or because you just don't like to believe in a religion that has fear in it?

"I don't happen to believe in hell," somebody says. Is it because you have come to an understanding of what the Bible teaches concerning it? Or is it simply that you don't wish to believe in it?

The wise man is telling us: "Let God be God; let Him define His own essence. Then decide whether you will worship Him or hate Him." For to change God is to make an idol. This is really the essence of idolatry. You go back to the Old Testament men of God. They do some things that we wouldn't dare to do. They actually argue with God. Look at Jacob: he wrestled with God and wouldn't let go until he got a blessing. (See Gen. 32:24-26.) Job was mad

91

at God. He said, "O God, am I some monster, that you never let me alone? . . . I would rather die of strangulation than go on like this" (Job 7:12,15,*TLB*). He argued with God. Jeremiah did the same thing: "Oh, remember the bitterness and suffering you have dealt to me!" (Lam. 3:19, *TLB*). The great writers of the Bible sometimes felt hostile toward God. They were wrestling with Someone who was real. They were willing to recognize their hostility and the problems that they had in relating to Him. But one thing they would not do, one thing they would never do. They would not dare to change the reality of the God who had revealed Himself, who had shown them His character and personality. They admitted they had a hard time accepting Him, admitted that they had a lot of doubts about the way He did things. But they would not succumb to the modern contagion of remaking God in their own image.

There is an analogy of acceptance that we talk about elsewhere. We say one of the problems in marriage is that one partner is trying to remake the other partner according to a certain image or expectation. The man says, "I think a wife should be thus, thus and thus. And it's obvious that you don't measure up, so the fundamental task will be changing you into my kind of a person." That's the direction of marital disharmony. If we hold rigidly to our idea of what another person ought to be, we pile on the tension and the friction until the other person behaves and conforms. Only he or she doesn't behave or conform. And as a result, we have the sundered marriage.

When we counsel people we try to talk about the

concept of acceptance. Throw away your preconceptions about what this person has to be. Accept that person for who he or she is. We understand this very clearly in our modern culture, as we attempt to heal the marriage relationship and the relationship between parents and children. Now when we understand this so well, why cannot we do this with God? Instead of making ideas about what God has to be, making up our own religion, why do we not let the God of Abraham, Isaac and Jacob be as He has declared Himself to be? To accept Him as He really is. This is a fundamental act of wisdom.

It's our unwillingness to accept Him as He is that engenders fear. We feel, "Here's someone I don't entirely understand; someone in whose hands I am totally helpless." That will create fear.

Someone has said, "I don't like this kind of God who has all these moral standards, this kind of God who gets angry with people who do the wrong thing." My friends, if you do not accept the power of God to condemn you, you will never believe in the power of God to forgive you. Until we accept the God who is there, not just the God we conceive in our minds; until we take Him seriously when He says, "Thou shalt not," we will never be able to take Him seriously when He says, "Thy sins be forgiven thee." And isn't that one of the most tragic and difficult experiences of our time? Even Christian people, who claim to believe in God, cannot believe it when God says, "Your sins are forgiven you." They still carry a mountain of guilt. Until we take seriously the wrath of God, we shall not really be solaced by the love of God.

93

The question is, "How can I know God?" The fear of God is the beginning of knowledge. This is the heart of the matter. You'll know Him, through wisdom. "I, Wisdom, will make the hours of your day more profitable and the years of your life more fruitful. Wisdom is its own reward, and if you scorn her, you hurt only yourself" (Prov. 9:11,12, *TLB*). This wisdom and knowledge is offered to any man, any woman, who will take seriously the reality of God.

How can we come to know the reality of God? The fundamental understanding of the first nine chapters of Proverbs is the perception that the wisdom of God is Jesus Christ. And in meeting Him, you experience God's love, His grace, and His forgiveness.

Lord, teach us that knowing God results in every other kind of understanding. And teach us, also, that the fear of the Lord is the beginning of wisdom. That if we are not made fearful in the wrath of God, we shall never be solaced in the love of God. That if we are not guilty before the righteousness of God, we shall never be cleansed in the forgiveness of God. For we ask it all in the name of Your dear Son. Amen.

footnote

1. For an elaboration of this view, see Theodore Roszaks's *Making of a Counter Culture* (New York: Doubleday and Co., Inc., 1969).

Winking at sin leads to sorrow; bold reproof leads to peace.

The good man's earnings advance the cause of righteousness. The evil man squanders his on sin.

The wicked man's fears will all come true, and so will the good man's hopes.

Proverbs 10:10,16,24, *TLB*

THE
WINK
OF
WOE

We have concluded the first nine chapters of Proverbs. They constitute a section of the book quite apart from the rest as an essay on the subject of wisdom. Now, with chapter 10, we move from an essay on wisdom to a description of the good man. Of course, there is a connection between the two. The good man is the wise man and the wise man is the good man. And there are references to wisdom and wise choices in the rest of the book. But the main emphasis is on the ideal of the good man rather than the concepts of wisdom.

The tenth chapter is a collection of proverbs. They are very difficult to string together, but three of the verses seem especially significant. "Winking at sin leads to sorrow; bold reproof leads to peace" (Prov. 10:10, *TLB*).

One of the structures of Hebrew-Semitic wisdom is to form a sharp contrast between the good man and the bad man. This we see well done in the couplet before us. It contrasts two things—sorrow and peace.

This verse is the opposite of the attitude that most of us possess. It appeals to a higher or more sophisticated kind of wisdom than that which we ordinarily practice. We want to avoid sorrow and to keep the peace. And it is precisely our desire to avoid sorrow and to possess peace that causes us to keep quiet over things we don't like, and to avoid any kind of confrontation. But this proverb seems to turn that over and to tell us that silence in the face of wrongdoing is going to lead us to sorrow, and the courage to stir up a little trouble by objecting is, in fact, what will lead to peace. Most of us are unwilling to recognize that the power of silence in the cause of evil is one of Satan's most formidable weapons.

We look at much of the evil and sin that is portrayed in modern literature or movies. We praise the ardor and candor with which "honesty" is portrayed. Somebody said to me recently that she thought pornography was one of the very honest things and that the church should become more honest. I wonder if pornography is really honesty, and if our silence is really detachment. Karl Olsson said in one of his editorials in the *Covenant Companion* that all this silent acceptance of honesty in literature and movies today would be all right if he didn't see a wink in the eyes of those who keep quiet. That wink betrays tacit participation. Silence is seldom neutrality.

Nor can we excuse ourselves by saying that we are not influenced by what we see on the screen or read in a book. The whole premise of our educational system is that what we read and hear and see does influence us. If that is not true, then we are wasting every dime we put into the public school system. Our silence in the face of many wrong values, our detached watching of horror and violence and illicit sex are nothing other than breeding grounds for the collapse of our society. Thus our leering silence, our "winking at sin," rather than leading to peace, as the world claims, will lead to sorrow, indeed to the very judgment of God.

How eloquent was the silence of the church in Germany. When Adolf Hitler was appointing his Reichs Bishops into leadership, when he was instituting his pogroms against the Jewish minority—how sweet was that phrase "The church ought to keep its nose out of politics." And it did. Except for the confessing church under the leadership of men like Martin Niemöller, the church was silent. It voted with its silence. The ravages of ten thousand bombing raids over the cities of Germany rained destruction not only upon the Nazis but upon a church that kept silent. God's wrath fell upon Hitler, but it also fell upon all the good people who felt that religion had nothing to do with politics or that they didn't want trouble.[1]

On the contrary, the wise man tells us, reproof means peace. Now don't get me wrong—I know a lot of people who always like to be brutally frank—or just brutal. I'm not talking about that person who likes holy justification for expressing his hatred. I don't believe in "honesty" that is just a pious excuse for knocking other people down. I think it's particularly despicable in the life of people who do this on the basis of their being holy. They feel they are the Lord's anointed prophets when they are really very hostile, troubled people who have found a pious excuse for inflicting their anger and hostility on others.

Proper reproof—healing, helpful reproof—comes from people who have no latent anger and hostility to displace upon others, who would prefer to avoid trouble, but who, for conscience' sake, realize that there are times when we must be willing to say what needs to be said. Businessmen—how often are you aware that criminal conspiracy is going on in meetings which you attend, and you simply think by being quiet you don't participate? You will be caught in that trap. Do you think you will jeopardize your job and your position if you speak up? So be it. Unemployment with a clean conscience is better than the memories that haunt you as long as you live even though you are never caught.

Honest reproof is the road to integrity even in marriage. I'm not saying you should blow your lid whenever your wife says something that you don't like. I'm simply saying that you have to learn the appropriate time and place and manner in which to express the reproof that is needed. Unless you can find a way to do this you will lose all your inner tranquility.

I once served on a committee which was trying to decide how a piece of donated property could be developed. The donor had some ideas about this building she wanted us to build, and we had an architect I was trying to lead to Jesus Christ. Nearly everyone on the committee felt the architect had done a passable job. But when he came before the committee to make his presentation, the donor decided to tear him up and down. I never thought anyone could talk that way. I hardly thought a stevedore could talk that way. And here we sat—three clergymen and seven dedicated Christian laymen—and waited with quiet patience. After all, the donor had given the property. After all, the meeting would soon be over and we would patch the guy up. So we all sat there in silence.

When we left, this man, whom I had counted a friend, said: "You mean you sat there and you let those things be said to me?" All our apologies did not undo what had already been done. And something closed in my capacity to communicate with this man that I could never rebuild.

I made a vow before God that I would never again be a participant in silence, as a part of a committee or as a human being where one person mercilessly attacks and destroys another. It taught me once and for all that winking at sin leads to sorrow, but bold reproof leads to peace.

The second couplet is Proverbs 10:16 (*TLB*). "The good man's earnings advance the cause of righteousness. The evil man squanders his on sin."

Let's take the second half of the couplet first. It is easy for us to misunderstand this idea of the wicked man. When I mention the wicked man squandering his money on sin you immediately think he goes to Las Vegas every weekend, or that he is a boozehound, or if he is under forty he is hooked on heroin. By thinking of these extremes we may all too easily dismiss the real significance of what the verse means. What the Bible really calls evil is not simply those horrible things which all respectable people avoid. Evil in the Bible is selfishness, the primacy of self-interest over love of God and neighbor. Thus we are to understand that the evil man is not just the man who spends his money on vice or who squanders his living on drugs and alcohol, but the man who lives a life of self-indulgence.

It is possible to be a good, honest family man, even a church man, and waste or squander our lives on self-indulgence. We can masquerade it under many causes, such as, "I'm doing this because it will create family security." Psychologists tell us that often what masquerades for love of wife and family may be a very exploiting relationship—a very selfish relationship.

In the final analysis, Jesus said the difference is not that we committed murder or theft or other grave sins. You remember the confrontation which Jesus described Himself having on the last day. He turns to the wicked and says, "Away with you, you cursed ones, into the eternal fire prepared for the devil and his demons. For I was hungry and you wouldn't feed me; thirsty, and you wouldn't give me anything to drink; a stranger, and you refused me hospitality; naked, and you wouldn't clothe me; sick, and in prison, and you didn't visit me" (Matt. 25:41-43, TLB). They ask how that can be, when they never saw Him to refuse Him these services. And He replies, "When you refused to help the least of these my brothers, you were refusing help to me" (Matt. 25:45, TLB). And He sends them away into everlasting punishment.

These are not bad people in the ordinary sense. They are simply people who forget that the main object of their lives is to alleviate suffering and to extend love to all men. It is precisely the sin that you and I practice so much of our lives.

You know, I think all of us, including myself, are secret believers in economic salvation. Ladies, have you ever said, "I know we can't afford it, but I have been feeling so down lately that I have to go out and buy a new dress"? Once I was feeling so badly when my wife and kids were away visiting relatives, that I said, "I've got to do something to make me feel better." So I went out and bought two azaleas to plant in my patio. Now what could be more devout and wholesome than planting a garden? The reason for planting the garden, however, was a subtle belief in economic salvation.

I realize that we all have to do some of these things; but how much of our lives are spent this way? We demonstrate our belief that happiness will come from the gain of some additional "thing." Now I'm not about to give up gardening as an act of personal piety; and I hope you ladies will not totally lose all interest in fashions; and far be it from me to encourage businessmen to go on welfare rather than to work. But how much of what we do is an attempt to buy economic salvation and a sense of well-being?

Notice the contrast: The evil man squanders his earnings on sin, while the good man uses his to advance the cause of righteousness. Evil is so powerful these days that we cannot define the good man simply as someone who avoids certain wicked things. The measure of the good man is the extent to which he commits himself to the cause of righteousness and invests his interest, his values, his time, his finances. This is a total commitment to the cause of righteousness. The good man's interests extend beyond the realm of his own personal security, they are global; they are even cosmic in their concern. When you give yourself totally to the cause of Christ, the cause of righteousness and goodness, then you'll experience joy in that kind of participation.

I am not saying you should join a committed church and double your giving, although it could include that. But what are we doing as human beings in the war on the drug culture? Merely shaking our heads when we read the newspaper in the morning? What are we doing about the problems in mental health? What are we doing about the difficulties of political corruption? About poverty? What are we doing about the two billion people who do not know Jesus Christ? What are we doing about our neighbors? What are we doing about the sad state of the Christian church?

"The good man's earnings advance the cause of righteousness." We're in a crisis today, and it is absolutely essential that those who are good do more than nod in approval on what's right and shake their heads in sorrow about what is wrong. We must have an army. It is essential that each of us be counted emotionally, financially and actively involved; otherwise we forfeit the right to be called good men. We have, to revert to my first point, voted for evil with our silence. And that inevitably leads to sorrow. For we in America will eat the bread of sorrow.

Now notice Proverbs 10:24: "The wicked man's fears will all come true, and so will the good man's hope" (*TLB*). Let's talk a moment about fear and hope. We all want hope and we all want to reject fear. What many do not see is the relationship between fear and sin, between dread and wrongdoing, and the inevitable fact that a fear is a self-fulfilling prophecy.

In the first chapter of Romans, Paul gives that incomparable although somewhat frightening account of man's iniquity and his state of deterioration. He has listed what evil men have done: "Their lives became full of every kind of wickedness and sin, of greed and hate, envy, murder, fighting, lying, bitterness, and gossip. They are backbiters, haters of God, insolent, proud braggarts, always thinking of new ways of sinning and continually being disobedient to their parents. They tried to misunderstand, broke their promises, were heartless—without pity. They were fully aware of God's death penalty for these crimes, yet they went right ahead and did them anyway, and encouraged others to do them, too" (Rom. 1:29-32, *TLB*).

Paul's statement is one of the most profound, philosophical statements ever penned about the nature of human conflict and why people act as they do. He is saying that every sin is done in the knowledge that it is worthy of punishment. This sense of guilt breeds more sin. This is what I would call the origin of pathological sin—the natural fears that are built into the human mechanism. It is built into the nature of the universe that the sins of men come back upon them. The liar is ultimately deceived. The adulterer is ultimately abandoned. There is no sin which a man may commit that does not come back to him as a sorrow. This is the origin of human fear. This is why the wicked man's fears will all come true. That which you fear most shall come back. The causes of evil will eventually be demolished, and you with them. As you cling to evil you rightfully fear your ultimate destruction. It is one of the most fundamental axioms of life.

On the other hand, the good man's hopes will all come true. That doesn't mean that good people don't get frustrated or never have problems. Look at Jesus on the cross. Look at Jeremiah locked up in prison. Look at Stephen being stoned. I don't insist on a simple, naïve interpretation of what the writers of the Proverbs said. But if it is true that through the power of God and the power of the Resurrection the good will ultimately triumph, then the man who hopes for a triumph of righteousness and love and peace will himself be triumphant.

Let me turn again to Paul. Here was a man who was nearly blind—who, tradition tells us, was a hunchback—a man whose family had thrown him out—a man who had lost one of the highest positions in the Jewish nation because of his conversion to Christ. He had lost everything—in a sense all he had hoped for. He experienced great unhappiness and disappointment. And when he became a Christian, the Christian church wouldn't let him in the door, they were so frightened of him. He was literally a man without a country. To his own nation he was a betrayer, and to the Christian community he was a spy.

He eventually rose to leadership and founded churches across the Roman Empire. But in every one of them there was dissent against him and criticism. In so many of these there appeared to be failure. He was imprisoned. He was beaten. He was left for dead. Three times he was shipwrecked. Finally he was taken off to Rome to be beheaded. And you say all the good man's hopes will come true? That man looked like he had lost. But hear him now as he writes some final words to Timothy, even as the executioner is sharpening his ax. Here is the man who sees it all. "I have fought the good fight, I have finished the course, I have kept the faith; in the future there is laid up for me the crown of righteousness" (2 Tim. 4:7,8, *NASB*).

Here is a man not living in the regrets of past failures, but a man with the sublime assurance that he has been a faithful servant of Christ. And off goes his head but on live the churches that he founded. Who will take his place as the greatest of all the interpreters of the Word and leaders of the Christian Church, save for the Saviour Himself? It could be said of Paul that, despite all his suffering, the things for which he really hoped have all been fulfilled; because in a crucial moment of life he was willing to abandon everything to follow Jesus Christ. And I invite you to do that, too.

> *"My hope is built on nothing less*
> *Than Jesus' blood and righteousness . . .*
> *On Christ, the solid Rock, I stand;*
> *All other ground is sinking sand."*
> *William B. Bradbury*

footnote

1. William L. Shirer, *The Rise and Fall of the Third Reich: A History of Nazi Germany* (New York: Simon and Schuster, Inc., 1960), pp. 234–240.

The good influence of godly citizens causes a city to prosper, but the moral decay of the wicked drives it downhill.   Proverbs 11:11, *TLB*

THE
CITY
AND THE
CITIZEN

The relationship of the citizen to the city is, basically a romantic relationship. It has all the elements of love, hate, conflict, and resolution that are found in the relationship of a man and a woman. Notice that we refer to cities as feminine. We talk about the city as a "she"—she's a great old town. I don't think we ever talk about a city as a "he." As a woman is either destroyed or ennobled by the man in her life, so a city is either wrecked or ennobled by the citizens in its boundaries.

Most of us are very aware of the peril of our cities, the crisis of our culture. This proverb seems appropriate for modern urban man.

The romantic relationship of the city and the citizen has several forms. *One is seduction.* It is entirely possible that the city in our time, as in ancient times, may be an element of destruction in the lives of those who court her. A biblical illustration of this is the story of Lot in Sodom.

Lot chose the plain in front of Sodom in which

to settle with his family and his cattle. As the days went by the magnetism, the beauty, the winsomeness of Sodom lured Lot to move his tents closer and closer to the city gates. Finally Lot was sitting in the very gates of the city, and his own children were seduced within its borders. In the end, Lot barely escaped with his life.

The Bible gives us a warning about the city's capacity to destroy us, despite its beauty. It can lead us away from God, lead us into paths of behavior which will involve us in the ultimate destruction of the city under the judgment of God.

This ancient fear of the city, which is with us even to this day, is vividly portrayed in the book of Revelation. A city is portrayed as a great harlot: "So the angel took me in spirit into the wilderness. There I saw a woman sitting on a scarlet animal that had seven heads and ten horns, written all over with blasphemies against God. The woman wore purple and scarlet clothing and beautiful jewelry made of gold and precious gems and pearls, and held in her hand a golden goblet full of obscenities. A mysterious caption was written on her forehead: 'Babylon the Great, Mother of Prostitutes and of Idol Worship Everywhere around the World'" (Rev. 17:3–5, *TLB*). The woman's animal is identified in verse 9: "'And now think hard: his seven heads represent a certain city built on seven hills where this woman has her residence'" (Rev. 17:9, *TLB*). It's Rome, the city of seven hills. Here we see the biblical picture of the city as seducer, as one who ultimately destroys those who fall into her trap.

The city is full of drama, intrigue, and opportunities. There is the vast process of urbanization, the moving from the agricultural areas into city life. And what happens when you have a mass migration as we had at the end of the nineteenth century to America's industrial cities? We have the slums. Today we see them in the developing nations throughout the world. There are hundreds of thousands, even millions, of people living in tar paper and tin shacks in the cities of the world. They come to the city with the promise of hope; and they are destroyed and reduced to tragedy within its perimeters. You can see this in virtually every major city of the world.

I think we all feel the tragedy of the city, the rise of crime and violence. People who work in the city move to the suburbs because they know that the city can be a treacherous thing. Then the suburbs get too crowded and people start migrating even further out to escape the seduction of the city.

The tragedy of the city also involves the basic destruction of Christian values. It is not strange that the Christian church is the most dead in the heart of our great cities. It has always been that way. The city seems almost inimical to devout life. It has a way of forcing us into conformity. Paul warns us, in the book of Romans, "Be not conformed to this world" (Rom. 12:2). The pressure to conform, to be seduced, represents the first mood in the romance between the city and the citizen.

The second mood is escape. I have already alluded to this. Here is the relationship in which one partner feels threatened and is busy trying to escape the clutches of the other. We see this mood well portrayed in the Scriptures. In Matthew 24, Jesus is talking

111

about the great destruction that shall overtake the city of Jerusalem. He tells the people to flee in that hour, not even to bother to pack anything or to turn back, just get out of town. Here is escape from the city.

Modern suburban life is one attempt to escape from the city. Another is to build a fort *in* the city. Many of the modern apartments in cities have locked gates and armed guards; residential areas are walled off. We fear more than the physical danger; we fear the emotional, moral and spiritual destruction of the individual in mass city life.

One of the most common escape responses in the Christian church around the third and fourth century was to flee worldly pressures by entering into monastic life. The first to try it were hermits. They were like some young people today who feel that the city is so corrupt that they have to escape to the countryside. Out of this move away from the city came the great monastic orders of the Middle Ages and those that survive even to this day.

The Protestant community doesn't go in for monastic orders very much. But we build church relationships so vital and so strong that virtually all our social relationships, other than business connections, are taken care of within the Christian community. I remember one of the leading laymen in a church, one of the most effective men that I knew, saying to me, "Pastor, as the years go by, I feel more and more guilty because more and more of my time is spent in church. When you tell me now to go out and witness and to lead someone to Christ, I discover that I know fewer and fewer people who aren't Christians." This can happen in the large city because you don't know your neighbors. Everyone is anonymous, until you find a group with which to relate. And by relating only to that group, you buy your safety.

But the romance between man and the city can move from seduction and escape to confrontation. One may choose not to escape, one may choose not to abandon it, one may choose to change the city. Did Paul say in his epistle to the Romans, "Be not conformed to this world, run out and join a monastery so you can escape contamination"? No! He said, "Be not conformed . . . but be ye transformed by the renewing of your mind" (Rom. 12:2). Leave your mark in the city where you are.

One of the most tragic assumptions is that when we escape from the city we escape from evil. You can't do it. You carry your own fleas on your back. Escape has never really been a satisfactory answer. It means you have to abridge the Great Commission. You have to forget about neighbor love in order to save your soul. And to do this is not to save your soul, but to damn your soul. If, in an effort to preserve our own purity, we repeal the Great Commission to make disciples of all men, we in fact become disobedient. There is no safety in disobedience.

We seem to believe that the city in itself is evil, and that small towns are great. This is not always true. Henrietta Mears used to say, "God made the country, man made the city, but the devil made the small town." If you visit some small towns today, you'll find that drug abuse and immorality are quite as bad in those communities and in rural areas as in the city. Holiness is not a country experience. Sin

113

is everywhere, and escape from the city is not escape from sin.

As a matter of fact, urbanization is part of the divine plan. I can prove it to you. The Garden of Eden was rural, right? But what is heaven? It is the City of God, the new Jerusalem. What does it look like? Look at the book of Revelation—it is a cube-shaped apartment house. Now I may be facetious, but I want to point out that this is a very significant fact. The final state of man is not a return to the garden, but to a city of God! So the city is not evil in itself. The city of God is called Jerusalem and the church which mirrors this is called the city of God. The city, while it contains evil, is also a part of God's plan for redemption.

It is interesting that Jesus did not stay in the beautiful Galilean countryside; He migrated to Jerusalem. And when He saw the destruction that was to come upon her, He wept over the city. "O Jerusalem, Jerusalem, which killest the prophets, and stonest them that are sent unto thee; how often would I have gathered thy children together, as a hen doth gather her brood under her wings, and ye would not!" (Luke 13:34). He loved the city. He went to the city. He lived in the city.

When Paul went to evangelize, he did not begin among the hill-country aborigines. He went to the cities, to Damascus, to Jerusalem, to Caesarea—and his great desire was to go to Rome, the greatest metropolitan center of his day. That's where the action was. That's where he wanted to live. That's where he wanted to be.

When you confront the city you stand in a very

biblical role. You stand in the role of a prophet. You do not enter the city as one who agrees with the dehumanizing, immoral, unchristian ethos that seems to rule it, and the way in which it grinds human beings and destroys families. But you stand as a witness against it. And this is part of the biblical response.

During the reign of Jeroboam II in Northern Israel, prosperity came in unprecedented measure to the land. But the people had forgotten about the poor. This is one of the tragedies of the city, that the poor become so anonymous and so often invisible. But God noticed, and He called a shepherd out of the countryside. His name was Amos; he was from the little community of Tekoa. God told him to tell the people that they must do justice by the poor. No more could they spread their lands field to field and house to house. (Sounds like subdivisions.) No more could they sell the poor for a pair of shoes. The whole book is Amos' denunciation of the people's callous treatment of the poor and the handicapped.

Because God cares, we stand for the poor and the oppressed and the sick. We have to take a stand on moral questions—and that can be very costly. John the Baptist wasn't one of those preachers who just stuck to preaching; he went to meddling. He went to King Herod and said, "It's not lawful for you to have your brother's wife. It's immoral." And Herod cut his head off.

I didn't say it was easy to be a prophet. I just said that the role of confrontation is a part of the biblical relationship between the city and the citizen. We have to be involved.

The great religious awakenings that have come throughout history, that have affected the cities and the civilizations, have come from men taking the prophetic role. Yes, John Wesley was a great evangelist; he was also a great social reformer. He and the rise of the Methodist Movement were responsible for the end of the slave trade, for reform laws, for justice.

Secular historians ask the question, "When France was undergoing the slaughters of the French Revolution, when it seemed the whole world was going to blow up in revolutionary anarchy, when the poor masses were slaughtering the rich, why did this not happen in England?" Certainly there was as much poverty and injustice and inequity. And secular historians, not just Christian historians, have concluded that the impact of Wesley and the religious awakening so changed the attitude of the nation that justice was restored in that generation. Through the witness of the Christian community, England was spared the horrors of a revolution. It was also through these awakenings that the American independence movement survived its early infancy.

The foundation of the movement against slavery was in large measure a spiritual confrontation. The great revivalist, Charles Finney, who was also a social reformer, was one of the leading abolitionists of his time. Even Wheaton College in Illinois was used illegally as an underground railroad to hide escaped slaves from their masters. Jonathan Blanchard, Wheaton's founder, was quite a man for civil disobedience despite his Quaker ways. He broke the law by hiding escaped slaves in the basement.

In the early days of this century the lot of the farmer

was very hard and the destruction of the small farm was at hand. Then William Jennings Bryan arose, and, in his famous Cross of Gold speech, denounced a monetary system which he felt worked against the working man, the small farmer, and the poor.

These were all movements of confrontation with the city. Moral reform, social reform, legal reform, medical reform are part and parcel of the Christian relationship with the city. Our most effective witness in evangelism comes when we are seen to be a part of the process of reform. Confrontation, then, is the third movement of the romance of the city and the citizen.

The final movement is courtship. There's a difference between confronting the city and winning the city. There's a difference between social action and evangelism. And while I can point out the great social reformers of the Bible and history, I also want to point out the great evangelists. They're never totally separate. Paul did not go to the city of Rome to set Caesar straight. He went to bear witness to the gospel of Christ.

If Christ is indeed the answer, then important as all of the social reforms are, the most important thing is the people and their relationship with God. After all, the city is people. And what is the morality of the city without the morality of the people? And what can produce morality but the grace of Jesus Christ? More important than any of these other things is the fact that men and women become new persons in Christ. We win them not through confrontation, but through the grace of Jesus Christ. That's courtship and there can't be any coercion in that.

There is a peril of too much confrontation and power in the church. When the church has moved too strongly to make itself felt in the city, and has actually taken over some of the power of the city, history has dealt unkindly with the church. Once she has seized power she has been subject to the same kinds of corruption as the city which she was trying to convert. It's a very sad history. We've burnt the heretics when we have had the power. We have denied the right of dissent. In the long run the church is not to be trusted with civil power any more than any other group, because it is ruled by sinful human beings. "Power corrupts," said Lord Acton, "and absolute power corrupts absolutely."

The greatest power of the church is not in the secular power she can seize in her confrontation with the city, but in the persuasiveness with which she can win men and women to discipleship to Jesus Christ. This is personal ministry: this is concern. This involves the kinds of concern you have for your neighbors and the people with whom you work. This is the ultimate mission to which we are called.

Father, we have thought of the romance of the city and the citizen. We sense all the perils of the city. Help us not to become conformed, seduced by the city to its standards. Save us, our Father, from escapist solutions. Teach us, our Father, that we must rather in the power of Christ confront the city, and be active in reform and progress and change. Help us to see that we are called to be persuasive in the courtship of human souls, that they may find salvation, and hence the city's renewal, through Jesus Christ. Amen.

118

It is possible to give away and become richer! It is also possible to hold on too tightly and lose everything. Yes, the liberal man shall be rich! By watering others, he waters himself.   Proverbs 11:24,25, *TLB*

11

PRODIGAL PENURY

At first glance these statements run counter to our ordinary experience and expectations. But if we look more profoundly, we will become persuaded of the reality and truth of these words. Once we understand that selfishness is the short circuit of human happiness, we can see that the only road to happiness is the road of liberality with our time, our talents, and our treasures.

This statement is, of course, paradoxical because you don't have more when you give something away. It violates all the rules of mathematics. But if I may quote one of the greatest mathematicians of our century, Lord Bertrand Russell: "Mathematics and logic have nothing to do with reality."

Having dispensed with mathematics and logic, let me proceed to Holy Scripture, and the paradox of the Golden Rule: "Do for others what you want them to do for you" (Matt. 7:12, TLB).

That idea makes some sense if we talk about a world that has not given in to the law of the jungle, or if we understand it simply as an ethical injunction—something that God expects of us.

But the book of Proverbs adds another nuance to the Golden Rule. It says that it's not only important to be liberal and generous with others because it's God's Law or it is the only way the world will work—but also because it's the only road to personal fulfillment.

Let's think of love as energy. Many of the great psychoanalytic and psychiatric theories build their understanding of emotional health and life on the concept of love as energy—the energy of life. The Christian affirms that God is love. And love is the great power. It is the only ultimate reality of the world.

Love is analogous to other forms of energy. Electricity, for example, only has value as it is transmitted through an appliance—something other than itself. Most of us who use electrical appliances are anxious to avoid having a short circuit. When the energy moves too quickly from the positive to the negative pole, without passing through an intervening resistance or appliance, too much energy is generated. That results in heat, fire, blowing a fuse, flipping the circuit breaker. Unless the energy passes through something beyond itself—to light a lamp, heat a room, cook a dinner—it becomes destructive. It destroys not only the appliance but its own avenues and channels for expression.

Thus, human selfishness, which is the concern to satisfy our own needs without caring about others, is in effect a short circuit. And its end result is destruction—not only in our society, but within ourselves.

He who waters others waters himself. If you wish to increase yourself, if you wish self-fulfillment, live a life of liberality and relationship and sacrifice for others. If you move immediately to self-satisfaction you will not find happiness, you will only find destruction. You'll blow a fuse.

Now there is one objection to this analogy that is often raised by ethicists—people who study questions of right and wrong. They object that it makes Christian ethics a form of sophisticated selfishness. I'm giving to others because I really want to "get" in the end. I'm being kind because it will make me happier to be kind, not because I care anything about the other person. A man says, "If the way to get rich is not to build more barns but to build churches, then I'll build churches—not because I like churches any better than barns but because it's a quicker way to get rich." Christian ethics become nothing but an indirect form of selfishness.

There is a certain amount of truth in this viewpoint, although we don't have to buy it completely. One can be very generous and find happiness in sacrificing for the cause of Christ and others, without ever realizing that he's contributing to his own happiness.

As a matter of fact, I think God has shrouded the truth of this with some ambiguities, so sinful men don't become too pious for the wrong reasons. I know a lot of holy people who are as poor as church mice, and who sacrifice their very lives for the cause of the kingdom. We must be wary of too naïve an

123

interpretation. Being kind and gracious and generous and sacrificing to others does not automatically add to our bank balance or expand the hours of our day.

But the truth is still there, if it is discerned. I should like to pose a corollary: the less conscious we are that our acts of generosity are contributing to our happiness, the greater the happiness that will come to us. The more happiness is sought for its own sake, the less it is found. The more it is sought for other people's sake, the more it becomes our fulfillment and our happiness, too.

Let me illustrate this with a simple example. My brother was pastor of a small church in Southern California when he was in seminary. One night an arsonist set the church on fire and burned the whole thing down. This included all of my brother's books and all of his sermon notes which he had been collecting for some years.

My brother was an addictive mimeographer, as some preachers are; he had been making copies of his sermons and outlines for the benefit of others. Because I was one of his nearest relatives I had a complete file of things that he had sent me. After the fire he said, "You know, the only thing I have of my past is what I gave to other people." As the saying goes: "The only things we ever keep are what we give away."

That is what our Lord Jesus tells us in the twelfth chapter of John's Gospel: "Jesus replied that the time had come for him to return to his glory in heaven, and that 'I must fall and die like a kernel of wheat that falls into the furrows of the earth. Unless I die I will be alone—a single seed. But my death will produce many new wheat kernels—a plentiful harvest of new lives. If you love your life down here—you will lose it. If you despise your life down here—you will exchange it for eternal glory' " (John 12:23-25, *TLB*). To phrase it another way, "Whoever wishes to save his life shall lose it; and whoever loses his life for My sake and the gospel's shall save it" (Mark 8:35, *NASB*). That is the paradox of the Golden Rule.

That leads us to a second paradox, the paradox of penury. It is possible to hold on too tightly and to lose everything. To be so concerned for our personal welfare that we end up paupers. This applies to every aspect of our lives.

Look at time. We say time is short. We haven't much time. The time must be given to my family; later on I will serve God. Later on, when I have met my obligations, I will give of myself for others and for His kingdom.

I'm afraid that another false value is the idolatry of the family. We recognize that the family is crucial in shaping children's lives, in helping them become the kind of people they should be. We recognize that the most meaningful human relationships are those that exist between husband and wife, and that if we are to have meaningful relationships and fulfillment, we must spend time together. This is true not only quantitatively but above all, qualitatively. It isn't so much how much time you spend together, but what you do when you are together. There's not much communication in spending four hours watching the "boob tube."

But our acute awareness of the importance of the family may become a trap. Our awareness of the crucial nature of the time we spend with our children may cause us to minimize our relationship with God and the time that we owe Him in the ministry of His kingdom. We hear the example of Deacon So-and-So, who spent seven nights a week down at church and his family went to Hell. See how bad it is to give yourself to God? Give yourself to the family, that's the only way to save it.

There are many people who do certain things, not because of a sacrificial spirit, but because they have neurotic compulsions. They are obsessive people. For this sort of person, church-going and involvement in church activities may be obsessive. They may arise, not simply from an authentic love for Jesus Christ, but from a form of obsession. Similarly, devoting oneself to sports events or to community activities can be a cop-out, an escape from grappling with other problems.

People with obsessions need help. But let's not use their problems as an excuse to idolize the family relationship to the exclusion of what we really owe to God. If the family is going to survive and our children are going to be the kind of children that God wants them to be, we must learn to "seek . . . first the kingdom of God, and his righteousness; and all these things shall be added unto you" (Matt. 6:33).

The three most active families in the leadership of my former church were families in which every one of the children knew and loved Jesus Christ and walked according to the will of God. Out of those three families there are now at least two ministers, and there will possibly be four.

If we have a lot of conflicts and inner personality

problems that haven't been worked out, let's not blame the church for the fact that we're losing our families. I remember one man who used to say, "I can't come to the meeting, because I owe my time to my family. The church is impinging on my family life." All three of his children wandered away from God because he did not honor God first and he did not teach his children to honor God. Jesus said, "If anyone comes to Me, and does not hate his own father and mother and wife and children and brothers and sisters, yes, and even his own life, he cannot be My disciple" (Luke 14:26, *NASB*). We must put God first. If we really do that, He Himself will direct us in giving our families the quantity and the quality of our time that they need!

The paradox has to do not only with our time, but with our talent. It is possible to hold on so tightly to our professional skills and gifts that we lose them completely. Just as a parent may clutch a child too tightly and lose him, so we may clutch too tightly to our career and vocation.

I think of an executive who is running into trouble: collisions with everyone, collisions with his supervisor, with his board, with his colleagues, with his employees. A colleague of his is a psychologist as well. These are the words that he used to describe that executive: "He takes his job too seriously, and thus he's doing it poorly. If he didn't count on it quite so much, if he could just let it be a job, he would be an excellent administrator. But because he clutches it so strongly and makes such a great emotional issue out of it, he's failing."

I've talked to a man who had given himself to

127

a job, and then came a conflict which left him on the outside. When he left he said to me, "Pastor, after all the years that I have given, I feel like a squeezed lemon rind. I have given myself so totally, but I was as dispensable as an orange peel, a lemon peel, or a peel of grapefruit. All that I had was taken out of me. And all I have left is a crushed shell."

I have another dear friend, now gone to be with the Lord, whose company demanded and demanded and demanded and demanded. He said, "Pastor, if I can make it one more year, I will be in a position to retire."

And I said, "Your heart can't take it."

He said, "But I must." And thirty days later he was dead.

I know of another man who always said he was going to make his money for God, but somehow that was always in the future. He said, "After I make my money, then I'll give to God. After God makes me a millionaire I'll pay Him a dividend." The collapse of his business brought to light his dishonorable business dealings, despite the fact that he claimed to be a Christian witness. It also involved scores of other people whom he brought down to financial ruin. It is possible to hold on too tightly and to lose everything.

There's a third paradox in our verse from Proverbs. Not only the paradox of the Golden Rule, the paradox of penury, but the paradox of liberality. "It is possible to give away and to become richer! . . . Yes, the liberal man shall be rich!" It is interesting to see how much time a man really has when he's got his values straightened out—when he's got God in the first place, and his family in the second place, and his vocation in the third place. He doesn't have to spend all of his time in fear and worry and distraction. He can live in the "now," because his fears of the future are gone.

Much of our thinking is spent in what the Gestalt psychologist calls "rehearsing"—just thinking about what are we going to do, what is going to happen. Rehearsing is an important part of life. It helps us avoid problems and mistakes. But some of us spend all our lives rehearsing and never get on stage. We never begin to live. Because we're so frightened of the future we spend more time in anxious daydreams than in anything else.

Jesus said the time to live is now. "Do not be anxious for tomorrow," He said. "Do not be anxious then, saying, 'What shall we eat?' or, 'What shall we drink?' or, 'With what shall we clothe ourselves?' . . . For your heavenly Father knows that you need all these things" (Matt. 6:34,31,32, *NASB*). Time to quit rehearsing and get on stage. You'll be surprised how much time you have.

I mentioned the three families who were so active in my former church. I don't know how they found the time to do as many things as they did, and yet to do so many things as a family. To enjoy life the way they did is a tremendous thing. You could tell as you sat in their homes that they did enjoy life. They had all the sorrows and tribulations that others had. But life was fundamentally an exciting experience for them.

What about a man's talents? Look at Moses. Think of the talent he had to give up to follow God. If he would have been only prime minister, and not the Pharaoh, his name wouldn't even have gotten on an Egyptian hieroglyphic. He gave up his secular position for the Kingdom of God—and his name stands for one of the great turning points of history. One could say the same of Paul, who left his career as one of the most promising Jewish legal scholars of his time. He said, "I have suffered the loss of all things" (Phil. 3:8, *NASB*). He lost his life and he found it.

What about treasure? You say, "I can see that other point, but, Pastor, you just can't take X number of dollars and subtract so much money and claim that you've made an addition." Well, when we started out I said that we'd have to dispense with mathematics and logic if we were to get down to the truth of giving.

I don't know very many wealthy men, but there is one whom I know very well. One day, we were talking about Christian stewardship, and this man said to me, "You know, I give away a great deal of money and I constantly hear people say, 'The reason he gives his money away is because he's got more than he can ever give away. He can talk stewardship because he's got one of the great fortunes of our time.' But let me tell you his story.

"I didn't inherit my money," he said, "I started out as a young lawyer. As a matter of fact, I couldn't make any money as a lawyer when I first started out—I had to clean offices at night to make it. But I remember the time when I was struggling and money was short. I had fifty dollars on which my wife and daughter and I could live for the next two weeks. That was all. I went to a missionary meeting. When the missionary said they needed something, before I realized it, I had put the entire fifty dollars in the offering plate. I went home to my wife to say that we didn't have anything to live on for the next two weeks. Even to buy food.

"And what I'm trying to say to you is that my fortune was amassed during the time I was giving my money away, not after. Before I die, I will have given away every cent of it." He literally believed this. It is possible to give away and to become richer.

Let me give you another illustration. A certain very wealthy man is a very dear and humble servant. When the church needed to relocate he went out and bought a huge piece of ground, and gave the church the finest section of it. In discussing this later he said, "I bought it for the church and I had to buy it in a big hunk or we couldn't get it. So I bought the whole thing and gave the church the prime part. I don't know what happened, but I made more than a million dollars off the rest of that land."

And he added, "I thought that it might be all right if I bought the piece of property across the road—and I've just signed the lease on it for one of the largest shopping centers in the state."

I don't want to create the idea that piety is the way to riches, because this story certainly is exceptional. If it weren't exceptional, I probably would not have used it. But it illustrates beautifully what the Scriptures tell us, that the only things we ever really keep are what we give away, and that selfishness is a short-circuit which will bring us to ruin.

Jesus said, "If you love your father and mother

more than you love me, you are not worthy of being mine; or if you love your son or daughter more than me, you are not worthy of being mine. If you refuse to take up your cross and follow me, you are not worthy of being mine. If you cling to your life, you will lose it; but if you give it up for me, you will save it" (Matt. 10:37–39, *TLB*). Such words are hard to accept and hard to believe. But they are the very heart of the Christian message. Jesus Christ is asking each of us to make that kind of commitment. We need to see the folly of selfishness, which can only short-circuit our happiness; we need to see love as an energy which only comes to life in the lives of others. We need to say, "Lord Jesus Christ, I want to put You first and I'll leave the question of my happiness in Your hands. You can do a much better job of making me happy than I can."

Father, the truth is so plain. And yet it is not obvious. It takes such an act of faith, such an act of sacrifice. Our hearts find it hard to really live this way. So grant us the grace through Your own Son, our Lord, to seek first Your kingdom and to put You first, and therein to find our happiness. Through Jesus Christ, our Lord. Amen.

Some people like to make cutting remarks, but the words of the wise soothe and heal. Proverbs 12:18, *TLB*

TALK
IS
NEVER
CHEAP

Words are never cheap. My statement contradicts that famous cliché "talk is cheap." The cliché is unbiblical, and also it is demonstrably false. Talk can be very costly.

There is a germ of truth in the old cliché, when we think of people who talk and never act. When talk becomes a substitute for works, then it is correct to say that talk is cheap.

But talk is not intrinsically worthless. It is talk that starts war; it is also talk, written on papers named peace treaties, that stops war. If you think that words are worthless, wait until you get that little sheet of paper in the mail that says, "Your long lost uncle left you one million dollars in his will." You will see how really costly talk can be. And how very, very precious. All the paper money in the world is nothing but talk on paper. It is costly because it represents the reality that stands behind it.

"Some people like to make cutting remarks, but the words of the wise soothe and heal." In some ways, cutting remarks can be more powerful even than sticks and stones. We say, "Sticks and stones may break my bones, but names will never hurt me." Anyone who looks back, however, will see that names do hurt—sometimes far worse than anything that is done physically. Seize a man in violence and maim him for life, perhaps even kill him, and his children and his community may raise a monument to him. But steal a man's reputation so that his children despise him, and you deprive him of far more than just his life.

Words are deadly, deadly things. They can set off wars and conflicts and produce great physical consequences. Words can powerfully destroy and shape. It is interesting to see what they do, not only to nations, but to marriages. Probably a wound worse than a physical blow is the statement, "I'm sorry I ever married you."

Whenever I do marriage counseling I like to talk to young couples about the deadliness of words, as well as their liveliness, their capacity to give life. I describe how to avoid the escalation of certain kinds of language which will always leave their scar. How many of you can never forget that a parent said to you in a fit of rage, "I wish you had never been born."

Words can be so terribly deadly. Psychotherapists

point this out. Most psychotherapy has simply to do with letting people talk. Words play a tremendous part in healing; many times not even the words of the therapist, but the words of the person who has been hurt.

Many of the Oriental religions talk about the ultimate reality being silence, the void, the ultimate, the unknowable, the indiscernible, the incommunicable. But Christianity doesn't talk about this void or silence. The first words spoken in the Bible are spoken by God. By faith we understand that the worlds were formed *by the word of God.* (See Heb. 11:3.) And when it comes to our very redemption, the One who came and brought us our salvation is the very Word of God made flesh. This is the biblical witness to the power and the significance of words.

How tragic it is that we have our tendencies to cut and to destroy with words, particularly when we Christians claim that we are people of peace and nonviolence. Some people like to make cutting remarks. What is that bizarre streak of cruelty within even the most devout saint that creeps out at times, that is as vicious as some man in a back alley with a knife, longing to draw blood from an innocent victim? What is it that makes us want to tell tales about someone else? Sometimes the very act of bearing those vicious tidings will cause more damage and more hurt than the evil we purport to tell. The lesser evil is supplanted by an even more vicious evil.

And we do this under the guise of piety and truth-telling! We like to be frank. We like to be honest. We like to be open. But in fact we enjoy our cutting remarks. How great to sit on Moses' seat and to pronounce our fellow human being to be less than he should be.

I want to be a wise man. I want to use the wise words which soothe and heal; which comfort a broken, wounded person; which try to put the best interpretation on any action. I want to be that kind of a man in the use of words.

The twelfth chapter of Proverbs puts an emphasis upon truth. "Lies will get any man into trouble, but honesty is its own defense. Telling the truth gives a man great satisfaction, and hard work returns many blessings to him. . . . Truth stands the test of time; lies are soon exposed" (Prov. 12;13,14,19, *TLB*). True words have great power; lying words are ultimately weak.

Here's a difficult point: true words are sometimes cutting words, and lies are sometimes soothing words. Now if we disapprove cutting remarks, and place great value upon soothing remarks, how in the world do we wed this with truth? Truth is sometimes a costly and a painful thing. One of our society's problems, particularly among those of us who have been in the adult years awhile, is that we have been afflicted with the theology of niceness. Be nice even if it's not true. Tell the lady that's the most beautiful hat you've ever seen, even though you wouldn't put it on your dog at a clown act. Tell her it's beautiful. Make her feel good. If you dislike somebody, don't hurt him by telling him that you dislike him. We have created a society which is so devoted to kind and soothing words, that it has substantially loosened its commitment to telling truthful words.

This is the struggle we have all the time, isn't it?

How to be kind and truthful, when so many times we are confronted with a situation where we have to choose between being kind or truthful.

One of the great criticisms of the Christian faith is that it says so many bad things about mankind. "All have sinned, and come short of the glory of God" (Rom. 3:23). "There is none righteous, no, not one" (Rom. 3:10). The words of Jesus so many times, to the religious establishment of the day, were anything but sweet, polite words. "Woe unto you, scribes and Pharisees, hypocrites! . . . How can ye escape the damnation of hell?" (Matt. 23:29,33). That's hardly soothing syrup. This is the dilemma that I have to face with the people in my congregation. Some are very wounded people, very hurt, bleeding people, on the brink of total despair. And some are hardhearted sinners who have set their teeth to defy God. How do you meet that kind of dilemma? Someone said the minister has an impossible job. His job is to comfort the afflicted and to afflict the comfortable.

To reconcile truth and kindness, we need to bring in another thought—the encouraging word. "Anxious hearts are very heavy but a word of encouragement does wonders" (Prov. 12:25, *TLB*). How may a man be both truthful and healing? How can anybody tell the truth and bind up the wound? To answer, we must turn to the center of history, to our Lord Jesus Christ Himself. Because it is He who came to bind up the wounds of the brokenhearted. But He also had the darkest words that were ever uttered to human beings who had hardened themselves in their sinfulness. Jesus is the very Son of God who came both to reveal truth and to heal mankind, to say that

139

truth and healing ultimately stand together. Not because they do so intrinsically, necessarily, or logically, but because Jesus took upon Himself our tragedy, because He suffered for our sin. And Jesus said, in effect, "The truth about you is that you have sinned. You have come short of God's glory. And the reason this cutting truth can be made into a healing truth is that I am going to suffer and die for you. I will take the suffering of those cutting remarks that you make, I will pay the price of the suffering which truth exacts. I will die for your sins."

A child who has broken a window must be confronted with the truth: the parent says, "I realize that you cannot pay for this. And I will bear the burden to restore what has been lost." Even so Christ says, "Look, let's be honest about who you are and what you have done." Standing by itself, that truth is destructive. Standing alongside the cross of Jesus Christ, that truth is redeeming. Because of Jesus Christ there is no truth about you that need destroy you. For that very truth, in the cross of Christ, shall heal you.

Oh, Christ, draw us to Your cross where truth and healing meet. Grant us the grace to see that the honesty of repentance leads to the healing of the soul through the blood of the Cross! Amen.

For whoever finds me finds life and wins approval from the Lord. But the one who misses me has injured himself irreparably. Those who refuse me show that they love death.

Proverbs 8:35,36, *TLB*

WISDOM AND THE DEATH WISH

Wisdom is speaking in this passage. She says that to reject wisdom is to love death. This is intelligible to most of us, except for the last phrase. While to reject wisdom is to court death or to stumble into death, it is difficult to understand that anyone could *love* death. It seems to most of us that the folly which leads to death is simply a mistake, because no person loves death. Yet the love of death, according to our text and according to what the Bible and modern science tell us, is often the cause of moral, spiritual and physical death.

That leads me to my first proposition, which is this: *death is no accident.*

Most of us are aware of suicide. Some of us have endured the tragedy and the sorrow of suicide in those close to us. A biblical example of someone who, in a sense, loved death, is found in the account of Samson. Shorn of his strength, blinded, fastened to a treadmill like an ox, a prisoner of the Philistines in Gaza, he labored as a beast of burden until he was brought to the great hall for the celebration as a trophy of the Philistine triumph over the Israelites.

In his sightless rage he wedged himself between two pillars which held the roof; he pulled them down, and the triumph of the Philistines became a nightmare of disaster.

But it is interesting to see that in literature and in the observations of anthropologists and physicians there are those who die, not through a deliberate act of violence upon themselves, but simply because they wish to die. The classical example of this is the voodoo death. An example is described in Melville's book *Moby Dick*. Queequeg was out on the water. He was a black mystic and he decided that he wanted to die, so he just sat down and died. He loved death.

Physicians tell us that many sick people fail to recover not because their disease or injury is so great, but because their will to live is gone. The individual chooses death. (In romantic suicides, love becomes so intense between two parties that in some perverse impulse both decide to commit suicide simultaneously as the highest act of mutual devotion.)

History has its share of romantic suicides. The German writer, Goethe, wrote a great deal of this. As a matter of fact a college friend of mine committed a romantic suicide as a result of reading Goethe. Goethe's writings were even banned in Germany for a time because they touched off a wave of romantic suicides.

All of this is just to say that there does exist within the human being not only a love for life but also a love for death. The man who first observed and described this phenomenon was the father of modern psychoanalysis, Sigmund Freud. He felt that there are two great forces or instincts in life. The one is Thanatos, or the death wish, and the other is Eros, the life wish. Thanatos finds expression in hatred, which ultimately turns upon itself and results in physical death. Eros is symbolized by the emotion of love and the seeking of unities with other human beings.

Freud tried to build his whole system of psychoanalysis upon this understanding of life and death. Modern psychiatry is based upon this dual instinct theory.

A famous book of our time is written by Dr. Karl A. Menninger, an active Presbyterian layman who is perhaps the leading living psychiatrist of our times. In his book, *Man Against Himself,* he describes the idea of the life wish and the death wish. This is what he says in his introduction: "In the end each man kills himself in his own selected way, fast or slow, soon or late."[1]

The book goes on to develop Menninger's concept of how the death wish ultimately triumphs over the life wish. The first category involves the deliberate acts of suicide. The second includes the "chronic suicides." These are people who do not realize that they are giving vent to their death wish. They subconsciously seek martyrdom, they practice asceticism, they practice invalidism (that is, they enjoy poor health; illness has become a way of life to them).

Addicts are in this category—the alcoholic addict and the drug addict. These people are giving expression to the death wish in the use of drugs and alcohol. They are really seeking death.

The death wish is found in antisocial behavior. We wonder why some people continually get into trouble

145

and seem to seek imprisonment. It is the love of death.

There are people who are accident-prone, those who have one automobile accident after another. They have a lifelong series of disasters, and it isn't just happenstance. There is something within them which seeks trauma and death.

And then Menninger develops a category of organic suicide, which he says is physical illness, which develops from psychological origins; the individual is giving vent to the death wish.

It's interesting that modern analysts are struck by the fact that psychiatry, particularly that of Freud, has given us a very good explanation of the death wish, but it has not given us a good explanation of the life wish, of eros, of love. Freud tried to explain it in terms of sexual relationships but even he got lost because he could not understand it. Erik Erikson has been critical of Freud for this failure. Erikson says that Freud was not able to give us a principle of life.[2]

The thrust toward death is a movement toward solitude and loneliness. The thrust toward life is a movement toward uniting with other human beings in the relationship of love, not simply sexual love as we popularly use it, but in all manifestations of longing for human and personal relationships. Dr. Menninger in his book, *Man Against Himself,* indicates the same sort of thing. He dedicates his book "To those who would use intelligence in the battle against death—to strengthen the will to live against the wish to die, and to replace with love the blind compulsion to give hostages to hatred as the price of living."[3]

Menninger concludes his book by saying, "Man is a creature, dominated by instinct in the direction of death, but blessed with an opposing instinct which battles heroically with varying success against its ultimate conqueror. This magnificent tragedy of life sets the highest ideal—spiritual nobility, in the face of certain defeat. But there is a lesser victory in the mere prolonging of the game. . . . It is here that science has replaced the magic as the serpent in the wilderness for the saving of what there is of life for us."[4]

Now let me pull that apart for a minute. He says, "Well, death is ultimately sovereign—it wins." There is, however, a life force within us that struggles, and for a time life can win over death. Science comes to the aid of life in this struggle. Menninger refers to the serpent in the wilderness. Back in the days of the Exodus, when the children of Israel were bitten by serpents and were on the verge of death, if they would look at the bronze serpent they were healed.

In the New Testament the uplifted serpent becomes a picture of Christ: "As Moses lifted up the serpent in the wilderness, even so must the Son of man be lifted up: that whosoever believeth in him should not perish, but have eternal life" (John 3:14,15).

Menninger says that science is going to replace that hope represented by the serpent. But all that science can give us, in the final analysis, is a temporary detour on the road to death's final victory. We may give our praise to the modern social and psychiatric sciences, but ultimately they are folly. The wisdom of this world is foolishness because it leaves death on God's throne.

147

That leads to the second thought: *to seek wisdom is to find the life of God.* Even the unbeliever, such as Freud, sees that there is a life force and that it is ultimately related to love and our capacity to relate to others. Here is common ground.

One of the most astute of the modern thinkers is a man by the name of Philip Rieff. In his book, *Triumph of the Therapeutic,* he says, "It is well to be reminded that love is the ultimate power."[5] Rethink that statement: If you look at the world it seems that death, not love, is the ultimate power. But Rieff, a modern thinker, says love is the ultimate power. He says that the psychotherapists need reminding of this and that perhaps once reminded, they will cease trying to repress "their own religious impulses. They are bound to become better therapists, at least less damaging ones."[6]

If love is the ultimate thing in the universe and not just a blind physical force, love can only exist in relationship between persons. This brings in the concept of a God who is love and is a person. And God is the ultimate reality. You can't believe in love as the ultimate without affirming that God is love. And since love seeks unity with other persons, you cannot affirm the reality of love and yet deny the personhood of God.

As we seek life and love and wisdom—as we find that wisdom leads us to God—we find that wisdom has a moral dimension to it. It recognizes that love is the ultimate value in life and that love is based on the integrity of relationships. Any lack of integrity in relationships is destructive of love.

Remember, that because love has to be honest,

the experience of love can be very painful. We risk a lot when we love. When you fall in love there's a terrible risk that the other person will not return your love, and that hurts. Love—the integrity of relationships—always involves pain; and to people whose fundamental emotion is the fear of pain, love is too high a price to pay.

When your hand goes numb, what do you say about your feeling? "It's *dead*." You don't feel any pain. Thus the fear of pain converts to the love of death. And what many people are experiencing unconsciously in their avoidance of relationships, in their retreat into solitude and inner dishonesty, is really nothing more nor less than the love of the grave.

The death wish seems to be what Milton put into the mouth of Satan in his *Paradise Lost*. It is Milton's effort to explain why Satan wanted to rebel against God. Milton shows Satan deciding that he doesn't want to be in a relationship where he has to worship God. If it means being Number Two, he doesn't want to be in a loving relationship with God. And so he says, "Better to reign in Hell than serve in Heaven." It is the love of death.

But some people move toward life despite the fact that life means pain. Think of the pain of our Saviour when you think of the love of God. He didn't draw back from life and love in order to avoid pain. He lived; He loved; He suffered for us in the world's ultimate act of love.

Paul talks about his own struggles with pain and with life and death. "Because of our preaching we face death, but it has resulted in eternal life for you. We boldly say what we believe (trusting God to care for us), just as the Psalm writer did when he said, 'I believe and therefore I speak.' We know that the same God who brought the Lord Jesus back from death will also bring us back to life again with Jesus, and present us to him along with you. These sufferings of ours are for your benefit. And the more of you who are won to Christ, the more there are to thank him for his great kindness, and the more the Lord is glorified. That is why we never give up. Though our bodies are dying, our inner strength in the Lord is growing every day" (2 Cor. 4:12–16, *TLB*).

There's the life wish, the love wish. We never give up because we see that even in our suffering we are growing. As Paul sees his body wither and grow old, as he sees death triumph over his outward man, he experiences that inner growth, that coming to life, that triumph of life over death. "But though our outward man perish, yet the inward man is renewed day by day" (2 Cor. 4:16, *KJV*). We never give up because of the triumph of life over death in Jesus Christ.

Paul tells us that although death is at work in us, death is not the origin of the universe, but an accident that has happened to man. He is saying that man's death is a result of his sinfulness, and the death wish is a symbol of sin's power to destroy us. Yet in the face of sin and death, the Christian affirms life. "For as in Adam all die, even so in Christ shall all be made alive" (1 Cor. 15:22 *KJV*).

And this leads me to my final thought: *To reject wisdom is to reveal that we have chosen to love death.* It is a question of choice. There is a moment in the soul when a person chooses to live or to die. Such a moment of decision came to the children of Israel. They stood before Moses and Moses put it to them simply: "Look, today I have set before you life and death, depending upon whether you obey or disobey. I have commanded you today to love the Lord your God and to follow his paths . . ." (Deut. 30:15,16, *TLB*).

Now notice, life is related to loving God. And love is related to obedience. "But if your hearts turn away and you won't listen—if you are drawn away to worship other gods—then I declare to you this day that you shall surely perish; you will not have a long, good life in the land you are going in to possess. I call heaven and earth to witness against you that today I have set before you life or death, blessing or curse. Oh, that you would choose life; that you and your children might live! Choose to love the Lord your God and to obey him and to cling to him, for he is your life and the length of your days. You will then be able to live safely in the land the Lord promised your ancestors, Abraham, Isaac and Jacob" (Deut. 30:17–20, *TLB*).

The crisis of the human spirit: Choose! The pathos of choice was seen in a nation that didn't seem to choose right. Centuries later, in the days of exile, the days of the prophet Ezekiel, God speaks in a pleading and plaintive voice. The people don't seem to want life. Everything they do seems to turn out to be wrong and leads to more destruction and disaster in the nation. They evidently love death. Ezekiel pleads with Israel: "Oh, turn from your sins while there is yet time. Put them behind you and receive a new heart and a new spirit. For why will you die,

O Israel? I do not enjoy seeing you die, the Lord God says. Turn, turn and live!" (Ezek. 18:30–32, *TLB*).

The words of God to Israel, whether through Moses or through Ezekiel, were addressed to everyone. Whether life shall win or death shall triumph is your decision.

Sometimes death comes very quickly. Years ago, there was a young man, an orphan fifteen years of age, up at a detention camp. I talked to him about the only hope in his life being Jesus Christ. I sat down with him the last day that he was in camp before being released. "You know that Jesus Christ is what you need," I said.

He answered, "I know that. I have no hope in life. My father won't have me because my stepmother hates me. I have no one in life. The patterns of delinquent behavior I have set have made the odds very poor."

I said, "Lad, are you ready to give your life to Jesus Christ so that you may live in hope?" His eyes fell; I looked at him for ten minutes. He never answered me. Finally he got up and walked away. Two months later he was found hanged by his neck from a tree on the lawn of Sequoia High School. He chose death rather than life.

For most, however, it is not open suicide. I came to the home of a man who had asked to see me. He said, "I am an unhappy man. I do not enjoy my work, I do not enjoy my wife, I do not enjoy my family, I do not enjoy doing anything. My life is one long everlasting depression." He said, "I know what you're going to say and I agree with you. I know that I can only find life and joy and fulfillment in accepting Jesus Christ. And I believe that what you say to me is true. But I will not do it. And I know that I go out into a life that is unhappy and miserable, but I will not." He was a man who had chosen to live by death. His was a living death, waiting only the hour when the death that he worshiped would claim him ultimately.

Why will you die? If any man refuses God, he shows that he loves death, but he that seeks wisdom shall find the life of God. Therefore, "seek the Lord while you can find him. Call upon him now while he is near. Let men cast off their wicked deeds; let them banish from their minds the very thought of doing wrong! Let them turn to the Lord that he may have mercy upon them, and to our God, for he will abundantly pardon" (Isa. 55:6,7, *TLB*).

Father, life and death are mysterious matters, and it is hard for us to recognize that perhaps there is within us more than a fear of death, but also a love of death. Help us to see that while modern science, in the forms of psychiatry and psychotherapy and psychoanalysis, can give us detours of hope and love on the way to death, they ultimately acknowledge the triumph of death. Father, help us to know that love is the ultimate, that You are love, and that in Your love You sent Your only Son. Amen.

footnotes

1. Karl A. Menninger, *Man Against Himself* (New York: Harcourt and Brace Co., 1938), p. vii.

2. Samuel A. Banks, "Dialogue on Death: Freudian and Christian Views," *Pastoral Psychology,* June, 1963, p. 46.

3. Menninger, *Man Against Himself,* dedication page.

4. Menninger, *Man Against Himself,* pp. 470,471.

5. Philip Rieff, *Triumph of the Therapeutic: Uses of Faith After Freud* (New York: Harper and Row, Publishers, 1968), p. 188.

6. Rieff, *Triumph of the Therapeutic,* p. 188.

**The path of the godly leads to life.
So why fear death?**

Proverbs 12:28, *TLB*

WHY
FEAR
DEATH?

"Why fear death?" This is, of course, a paraphrase. I think the words, "the terror of death," may convey the meaning more appropriately than "the fear of death." The fear of death is a natural, God-endowed fear within the human life. There is an element of fear regarding death that ought not to be taken from us. God put the fear of death in us so we wouldn't walk off cliffs just to see how fast we can get to the bottom. And so we wouldn't dive down to the bottom of the sea just to see what it was like down there. It teaches that hopscotch ought to be played on the sidewalk and not in the middle of the freeway. The fear of death is a very natural and important thing.

More than that, it appears that the fear of death is something which was found in our Lord Jesus Christ who was sinless.

In Matthew 26 we see Jesus contemplating death. He is deeply troubled. Call it fear or whatever you want. Theologians are inclined to say, "He wasn't thinking of His own death or His own suffering. He was thinking of all the suffering of all the people of the world." But I think this is to spiritualize Jesus entirely too much, for He was a man of like passions as we are. Jesus found suffering as painful as you or I do; He found the difficulty of submitting to the helplessness of death quite as unnerving as you and I would find it.

Jesus wept at the tomb of Lazarus, not because He didn't believe in the resurrection, but because he saw death as a tragedy and a hard experience, not only for Mary and Martha, but also for Himself.

I want to talk to you about how to avoid not the fear of death, but the terror of death. Something happens to the human personality as it contemplates death; ordinary fear is transmitted into terror. Fears are natural, but something can happen which makes people utterly terrified in the face of what is inevitable for every one of us, pending the return of our blessed Lord.

Many people don't think about death. Some say they are not afraid of it. But this is an evasion. Psychologists tell us that the fear of death is one of the most important components of the human personality, and that most of us erect around ourselves myths of immortality. Now I am not talking about the resurrection of the Lord Jesus, but an emotional attitude that says, "I'm going to live forever." We do this by suppressing the thought of our death. There is a morbid avoidance of the thought of death in many people, even as there is a morbid preoccupation with death in others.

Psychologists, many of whom are not Christians at all, say that one of the most important things that an individual must do in his life is to come to terms with dying. If we don't—we lay foundations for emotional illness. The fear of death can affect other areas of our lives without our even realizing it.

The writer of the Proverbs is in line with all the teachings of Scripture which show that the godly life is the road whereby we may learn to cope with the fear of death and keep it from turning into terror. "The path of the godly leads to life. So why fear death?"

The terror of death is connected with anxiety about the future. Anxiety is dread concerning an uncertain future. As Dr. Fritz Perls says, it is "stage fright."[1] It is the recognition that we might fail—that we can't handle something in the future. This terrifies us. Most of us say, "Now what is it going to be like to die when it's getting darker, the pain is getting worse, things are fading away, things are getting cold?" How many times have we rehearsed this little act? Many of us say, "I hope it happens when I'm asleep and can't even prepare for it—or it happens suddenly in a crash so I can't worry about it."

But let's push this a step further. Anxiety about the future and our death in the future is related to the origins of anxiety. It is the price we pay for our self-centeredness. If we are the center of our universe, then we have to run our universe. We have to take on God's prerogative. As long as we're building our own little world, we have to keep track of everything and we have to manipulate and control. Ultimately, of course, it's a failure because we don't control our lives. Most of us would be shocked if we knew how little of our lives we really control. People are so outraged today by B. F. Skinner's book, *Beyond Freedom and Dignity*. They say, "Oh, what a horrible beast—he's against freedom and democracy, religion and everything that's precious. He's going to lead us into fascism despite his prestigious position at Harvard. He's a thoroughgoing behaviorist." And I quite agree, but the fact of the matter is that he is mostly right (and mostly is the word I would underscore). As a Christian I would say there are significant times in life when God gives us real freedom, when He sets before us life and death. We can choose. But most of the choices we make are not free. They are determined by our background and our upbringing and the circumstances of the moment.

Anxiety arises when we begin to suspect that we are not really in control of our world. And there is nothing that so eloquently witnesses against the idea that we can build our own life as the idea of death. Life is jerked from us, willy-nilly. Our wishes or our desires have nothing to do with it. Because we are so helpless in the face of death when we have decided to build our lives around our own values, death becomes the ultimate enemy. It does not ask—it does not consult. It cannot be manipulated. It becomes the ultimate destroyer.

However, if you put yourself in the hands of God, you put yourself in the hands of Someone who has the keys of death and hell. You're in the hands of Someone who can be trusted, Someone who can make a bond-slave out of death, Someone who can make death a doorway to fulfillment.

I remember how depressed I was at the death of one of my dear friends. It made me really angry with

God. And then it seemed that the Holy Spirit spoke to me and said, "You've been looking at this from a self-centered viewpoint." The man had a great deal of suffering and one nervous breakdown after another. He was one of the great Christians of our time; my wife and I probably owe him more spiritual debt than any other man.

And the Spirit spoke to me in this fashion, for I believe it was the Spirit: "Here is a man whose life was filled with suffering. The tremendous creation of his mind and his spirit before he was forty-five years of age was what few men have done in a lifetime. And yet there was a heaviness and a sorrow that he just couldn't recover from emotionally." And one day God said, "I don't want to see you suffer anymore. Come home to Me." When I could look at his death from that perspective, I knew that death came not as an enemy to this man, but as a friend. It lost its terror.

That experience helped me to look toward my own death, whenever it shall come, not as an enemy—perhaps not as a friend whom I shall embrace willingly, but at least as a servant who shall lead me to a better place. That helps.

One of the things that compounds the terror of death is the memory of the past. You remember the famous soliloquy in Shakespeare's *Hamlet:* "To be or not to be: that is the question." The man is handling a dagger; he seems to be contemplating suicide. But as the soliloquy continues, he comments, "Thus conscience does make cowards of us all." He chickens out—he can't do it.

What is it that makes us chicken out? What holds

back our hand from suicide? It is conscience . . .
the past . . . guilt. The sense of guilt is one of the
strongest elements in turning the fear of death into
the terror of death.

Some may claim that this is just superstition. But
the idea that a man is accountable, that he must
answer for what he has done, is at the heart of the
Christian faith. In fact, it seems to be woven into
the warp and woof of all cultures. The sense of shame,
almost more than anything else, contributes to terror
in the moment of death and in the anticipation of
death. A person realizes, "I have done wrong . . .
I have sinned . . . I have displeased God."

You won't wipe out the sense of shame by telling
man that there are no moral absolutes. You won't
wipe out the terror of death by telling man that death
ends it all, that there is no life after death. You will
take care of man's conscience only by providing forgiveness.

Only a sense of profound and deep forgiveness can
prevent the sense of guilt which aggravates the fear
of death. The problem with many of us is that, while
we believe in the forgiveness of sin in our heads,
that forgiveness has gotten no farther than our heads.
We have no really deep, releasing, emotional, spiritual
sense of the forgiveness of sin—no assurance that "I
am a forgiven child of God, and despite my failings,
I'm okay in the sight of God."

If you want to learn how to handle your death,
learn how to handle the sense of guilt which you
possess now. Don't think that you can get by, kicking
yourself and downing yourself all the way through
life. Downing yourself is not a Christian practice,

because it essentially denies that Christ's death did anything for you. It is an act of unbelief. It is a substitute for the sacrifice of Christ. You don't have to die a second time for your sins. Neither do you have to suffer for them. Deal with that sense of guilt while you're in the prime of life because it will not only make your present life more meaningful but will tend to make death more manageable.

"The path of the godly leads to life"—and that means life *right now*. Oh, yes, it leads to life in the future—but we don't have to worry about that because God is the center of our future. God is in our past, too, through forgiveness in His grace. But in the present He has come to give us life.

People speak of death in many different ways. We may say of someone who's had a very rough life, "Well, death must have come as a blessing after all that misery over the years. He must have really looked forward to it." Or we say, "That death was such a tragedy. It was so sad because he was in the prime of life and he seemed to love life so much. Death was really terrible."

These ideas are absolutely false. The people who have grumped and miseried their way through life are those who die the most frightened and scared. Those to whom life has been the most exciting and fulfilling are the very ones who seem to be able to face death the most calmly. The old rule says, "Sour in life—sour in death; joyous in life—joyous in death." Some people think that if they get sour enough about this world they won't mind going to the next. That isn't the way it is. Sourpusses don't enjoy death anymore than they enjoy life.

"The path of the godly leads to life" in the here and now. It's a special quality of life. A person who has poured out his life in sacrifice and love to God has built relationships not only in this world but in the world to come. A person who has found Jesus Christ the exciting center of his life now is not inclined to go into total collapse at the thought of meeting his Maker.

Paul says, "For to me to live is Christ, and to die is gain" (Phil. 1:21). Got it? It means that I find life here and now. Now I realize the godly man may get put on the rack. He may be tortured. He may be afflicted with disease. God does not inoculate Christians against cancer or the bubonic plague. He does not put angels around us so we can never be hit by automobiles. He only assures us that whatever happens to us is in His will. The path of the godly person is a life of fulfillment. It doesn't mean that we have less pain than others. We may even experience more pain because we are caring about others and their pain may become our pain. It doesn't mean we'll have less physical sickness. Of those missionaries that went out as pioneers in the nineteenth century, eighty per cent died before the end of the first term. That doesn't mean that God didn't care about them.

It doesn't mean that you're going to live longer. Jesus died when He was thirty-three. But that has nothing to do with the quality of life, for the quality of life is not measured by the duration of its days nor the absence of pain, but by the fulfillment of love and of joy.

That is exactly what a godly life is. "The path of the godly leads to life." It not only leads to life, but it is a life stripped of the terrors of the death that may lie ahead, and the terrors of guilt which torment and aggravate. We can live in the moment. We can find life here and now. There is no life but the godly life.

We know that, but many of us have not settled the question of the priority of Jesus Christ. For that reason we remain afflicted with the terrors not only of death but also all the other anxieties in our present life. There is no happiness in a distant walk from your Saviour. There is no pleasure or fulfillment in a religion which has second place in your priorities. There is no joy without a total surrender to the Lordship of Jesus Christ.

Father, help us to be honest about our fear of death, to see now natural it is. Help us to see that how we deal with the question of death is important to our total life. And give us the insight and the grace to so deal with our past and our present and our future, that our fear of death shall not be escalated into the terror of death. In the end, may we experience death triumphantly, not as a conquering enemy, but as a conquered servant, who, shackled by the love of Christ, leads us gently into His everlasting presence. Amen.

footnote

1. Joen Fagan and Irma Lee Shepherd, eds., *Gestalt Therapy Now: Theory, Techniques, Applications* (Palo Alto, Calif.: Science and Behavior Books, Inc., 1970), p. 16.

To despise the poor is to sin.
Blessed are those who pity them. . . .
Anyone who oppresses the poor is
insulting God who made them. To
help the poor is to honor God.

Proverbs 14:21,31, *TLB*

OF
LAZINESS
AND
POVERTY

The Word of God has much to say about laziness
and poverty. They are in some ways related, but in
other ways unrelated; we must be very careful that
we relate them in a biblical way. There is an orthodoxy in American culture, even American Christian
culture, which says that no one needs to be poor.
This idea is born of our Puritan ancestry. It is born
of the great providence that God has given us in
this land, which is called the land of opportunity.
On the Statue of Liberty are penned the words of
Emma Lazarus:

"Give me your tired, your poor,
Your huddled masses yearning to breathe free,
The wretched refuse of your teeming shore,
Send these, the homeless, tempest-tossed, to me:
I lift my lamp beside the golden door."

And so the poor have come, and out of the wilderness has grown the mightiest nation on earth. America has become the inheritance of the poor and the dispossessed. It is often said in this country that any who are poor are poor simply because they are lazy. Unfortunately this half truth has come to be understood in the popular mind as a Christian maxim, but it is not a Christian maxim. It is a denial of the Word of God. Jesus said, "The poor you have with you always" (Matt 26:11, *NASB*). This has been misused by preachers to say that welfare programs are evil. But that abuse of the statement does not detract from the truth of it. There will be poor people as long as we live on this earth.

We must be careful not to condemn people categorically; but I don't want to say there is no connection between laziness and poverty. There often is. The book of Proverbs itself says so.

"Take a lesson from the ants, you lazy fellow. Learn from their ways and be wise! For though they have no king to make them work, yet they labor hard all summer, gathering food for the winter. But you—all you do is sleep. When will you wake up? 'Let me sleep a little longer!' Sure, just a little more! And as you sleep, poverty creeps upon you like a robber and destroys you; want attacks you in full armor" (Prov. 6:6-11, *TLB*).

There is at times a connection between poverty and the sin of laziness. Notice Proverbs 18:9: "A lazy man is brother to the saboteur" (*TLB*). Don't we say our welfare lists are bankrupting us? And Proverbs 19:15: "A lazy man sleeps soundly—and goes hungry!" (*TLB*). A lazy, chronically unemployed man was asked, "How are things going?" He said, "Ah, things are rough. I sleep all night fairly well, and in the morning I can make it, but in the afternoon I just toss and turn."

"Some men are so lazy they won't even feed themselves!" (Prov. 19:24, *TLB*). Perhaps the strongest words of the Bible on this subject come from Paul: "He who does not work shall not eat" (2 Thess. 3:10, *TLB*). That puts it pretty strong. Somebody describing our time said, "You know, people just don't want to work anymore." To which a waggish friend replied, "They never did, but now they won't."

The curse of sin is not labor; it is the anguish of toil. When God put man in the Garden of Eden He did not put him on a trout stream to float lazily down the river. He told Adam to cultivate the Garden. Man is created in the image of God, created to work; he is a laborer. Jesus said, "My father worketh hitherto, and I work" (John 5:17). When we labor we stand in the image of God in a very significant sense. Even the glimpses of heaven given to us in the Bible describe the saints' everlasting joyous service. Heaven is not a celestial retirement home.

We must acknowledge that laziness inevitably issues in poverty. Not only in the material sense, but also in the spiritual. There are many people who sense their material needs and labor like beavers to meet them—but they slumber through the worship service every week. They fail to see that spiritual laziness in the service of God and in the discipline of the heart will result in spiritual poverty.

While it is true that laziness will inevitably lead to poverty, it is not true, even in American culture, that all poverty is the product of laziness. Jesus was born into poverty. It was Jesus who said, "Blessed be ye poor" (Luke 6:20). In America's materialistic middle-class culture we have virtually equated poverty with sin. Yet nothing could be less biblical. "To despise the poor is to sin" (Prov. 14:21, *TLB*). Middle-class people have more trouble than upper-class, because we hate that from which we have been most recently delivered. "Anyone who oppresses the poor is insulting God who made them. To help the poor is to honor God" (Prov. 14:31, *TLB*). This is no socialist manual, this is the Word of God. "God doesn't listen to the prayers of men who flout the law. Income from exploiting the poor will end up in the hands of someone who pities them. . . . If you give to the poor, your needs will be supplied! But a curse upon those who close their eyes to poverty" (Prov. 28:9,8,27, *TLB*).

Poverty is often something that happens to people, rather than something they cause. For instance, many times we confuse the torpor of poor people with laziness. We do not realize the extent to which malnutrition can affect one's metabolism and energy level.

We fail to see that the poverty level of aged people in America is one of our biggest social problems. You can't help it if you are getting old! Social Security isn't adequate. One of the biggest scandals in our land involves the private pension plans of companies and unions. A congressional committee once concluded that eighty percent of the people who get involved in these pension plans never collect a dime.

A man in my former church was sixty days from retirement. He decided, since there had been a strike, to work that extra sixty days in order to get the full retirement. Four days from his goal he dropped dead. If he had made it, his wife would have had half his pension, but she got nothing. You can't say that she was poor because she was lazy or because her husband was lazy. It was the very industry that drove him past his physical endurance. In his desire to help her, he impoverished her.

I knew a dear woman in Pasadena who lived on a meager "pension," as she called it, but known as welfare by those of us who pay the taxes. The sole surviving charter member of our church, she was in her eighties and had lived that way for years—in dignity. This woman, who worked as a domestic all her life, was honored as one of the saints of the church she had been a part of for so long. I thank God that I can pay taxes so that somebody like her doesn't have to be reduced to utter degradation.

We also have to see that poverty can be caused by cultural background and discrimination. A former refugee in my church said to me one day, "Pastor, I have a hard time understanding all these black people being so poor. When the massacres came in my country, my family and I were stripped to nothing. I lived in a tar-paper shack for two years. Then we immigrated to this country and we have all been able to make it. Anybody with any drive would be able to make it if they want to."

This man was overlooking the vast differences between his experience and the black experience. His family had education; the black slaves were deliberately kept uneducated, and their descendants have suffered discrimination in education ever since. My friend's family stuck together; the blacks were kidnapped away from their families in Africa and sold away from their families in America. My friend and his family were able to work with the hope that they could better themselves; the blacks were forced to work to the point of exhaustion with never a hope of any benefit to themselves.

Finally, my refugee friend does not have black skin. And so he had many opportunities open to him which the white men absolutely refused to permit the black men. Discrimination in education, in housing, in employment has been the boot on the black man ever since he threw off the shackles of slavery. No white man can ever fully appreciate or understand that experience; no white man should have the audacity and lack of understanding to compare his own progress with the plight of a black man.

A highly significant factor in poverty is hopelessness. There is no way out. And when people feel there is no hope, no way out, they just quit trying. It is this mood of hopelessness that is the vicious cycle of the poor. "We'll never get out—never get out."

Into this kind of hopeless, self-perpetuating poverty, Jesus comes. Even where poverty is the result of sin, remember that Christ loves sinful people. The same mercy which we covet from God with regard to our sins, we must also be willing to share with those who seem to lack the virtues of industry and thrift and good manners.

What response can the Christian community make

to poverty? The church has been involved, though never as much as it should be, in feeding and clothing the poor. It does no good to say to a man, "Be filled with the spirit," when he has an empty stomach. Or, "Be clothed with righteousness," when he has no clothing. The poor of our communities are people to whom we must bring the message of love, which will come in terms of meeting both their physical and their spiritual needs.

Secondly, we Christian people must involve ourselves in the processes of government which will enable us more adequately to care for the poor. In Proverbs we see that God holds the king accountable if he lets the poor people go hungry and doesn't hear their cry. And in a democracy God holds the rulers accountable—and that's us. The Christian who says, "I want nothing to do with politics, I'm not interested in that sort of thing, it's all a waste," is going to be as accountable to God on the last day of judgment as the king who neglects the poor. We are accountable for the people for whom we vote, and for the fact that we even bother to vote.

The Christian is concerned about nutrition and feeding the poor. In the Old Testament law you had to leave the edges of the field unharvested so the poor could have the grain. That was an Old Testament welfare law. You could not allow people to go hungry.

I do not mean that Christians should always vote for more and more welfare laws. The Christian church must be humble; the fact that we are concerned about the poor does not make us authorities on the social and economic systems by which we may achieve adequate care for the poor. It appears that many of our present welfare laws are producing the very reverse of what we are trying to do. The all-or-nothing approach to welfare is actually discouraging people from getting jobs. We need to have programs that prevent the perpetuation of poverty.

We need to be concerned about our welfare programs—but not with the motive of avoiding paying for poor people. That is not a Christian motivation. We can thank God that we can be taxed to help the poor. But we can be concerned about the adequacy of current programs. Are we really doing the maximum good with the money we are spending?

There is something only Christians can give to the poor. I talked before about the cycle of hopelessness. When you put someone on the dole and you keep him there, you merely perpetuate the hopelessness. This is the tragedy of the chronic dole. It makes a person feel like a parasite. It diminishes his self-image in the long run. But we can bring into people's lives the Christian message of hope and the encounter of love. If a man can begin to hope that in Christ he is somebody, even though he is poor, we have planted within him a spark. With the help and assistance of his fellow Christians that spark will enable him to climb out of the misery and hopelessness of his estate. Loving evangelism is the foremost road out of poverty.

This can be demonstrated on the mission field again and again. You go to the poverty cultures and you reach the people and instill within them the love of Christ. You mobilize them and train them. The second generation of Christians on the mission field are almost inevitably middle class. Why? The educational interest of the missionary is important. But the essence of it is that the message of love and hope in Jesus Christ generates hope; and where there is hope there is deliverance from the shackles of poverty.

We must do more than vote new welfare programs; we must do more than have Thanksgiving baskets and food commissaries. We must bring the gospel to the poor. "Blessed be ye poor: for yours is the kingdom of God" (Luke 6:20).

Father, help us to understand the poor, to love the poor, to seek the poor, to feed the poor. Help us to labor unceasingly for changes in our culture and society which will ameliorate the tragic lot of the poor. Most of all, grant that we may be like the Lord Jesus, who came and said, "The poor have the gospel preached to them" (Matt. 11:5). In the name of Him who, though He was rich, for our sakes became poor, we pray. Amen.

Plans go wrong with too few counselors; many counselors bring success.

If you profit from constructive criticism you will be elected to the wise men's hall of fame. But to reject criticism is to harm yourself and your own best interests.

Proverbs 15:22,31,32, *TLB*

CHRIST
AND
CRITICISM

Sometimes it is hard for us really to feel the truth of the words, "It is more blessed to give than to receive" (Acts 20:35)—except when it comes to criticism! Then we would much rather give it than receive it. However, we must recognize that we need criticism. "If you profit from constructive criticism you will be elected to the wise men's hall of fame. But to reject criticism is to harm yourself and your own best interests."

We are blind to our own faults. The psychologists can tell us about the mechanisms of self-delusion. The Old Testament talks about people who have eyes but do not see, and who have ears but do not hear. (See Ps. 115:5,6.) Self-deception is one of the easiest and most common phenomena of human behavior.

Only through a process of counseling or criticism can we bring a person to the truth about himself so that he can modify his behavior.

Notice Proverbs 16:2 says, "We can always 'prove' that we are right, but is the Lord convinced?" (*TLB*). The greatest gift that God can give to the Christian is other human beings who can't always be convinced either.

One of our biggest areas of blindness is the myth of maturity. We think we are mature because we are adults. But we ignore the fact that our behavior is not always mature. We say that a child is immature if he yells when we correct him, right?

"You can't do that anymore."

"Waaah, I'm gonna do it, I'm gonna do it."

He's immature. But why don't we call it by the same name when adults do it?

We think that the only compensation for a balding head, sagging jowls and a fallen chest is the claim that we are mature. There is, however, a very small distinction between being mature and overripe.

The apostles who were the foundation of the Christian church, who were grown men, who later distinguished themselves as leaders beyond peer, constantly had to be corrected and upbraided by the Lord. Many people today think they have long surpassed the apostles in their maturity and that they need no assistance from anyone.

Peter got into a controversy about Christians following Jewish dietary laws. Even though he was the first of the apostles and their leader, he had to have a session with that man never noted for his tact—the apostle Paul, who records, "I withstood him to the face, because he was to be blamed" (Gal. 2:11). And you know what Peter did? He took it, and that was the greatness of Peter. He accepted the criticism; he modified his behavior.

Once we accept the need to be evaluated, Proverbs tells us a great deal about the danger of loveless criticism.

"A soft answer turns away wrath, but harsh words cause quarrels." "Gentle words cause life and health; griping brings discouragement." "The Lord hates the thoughts of the wicked but delights in kind words." "Pleasant sights and good reports give happiness and health" (Prov. 15:1,4,26,30, *TLB*).

We will discover that, needed as criticism is, it often comes in unloving, unkind, and hostile fashion, arising more from an individual's need to express hatred or resentment than from a desire to bring constructive and positive change in a person's life.

One of the biggest problems we face in family life is the destructiveness of the criticism by which husband or wife endeavors to reform the other. We wonder why we spiritual people sometimes drive our spouses from the side of Christ. We wonder what stiff-necked pride has caused our spouse to lose interest in church. But the stiff-necked pride was—not in the spouse, but in the self-righteous hypocrite who felt he must dispense the criticism!

One of our problems in America is that we have entered into an orgy of national self-criticism. Sociologists are saying that we have so lost confidence in ourselves and have subjected everything we say and do to such criticism that we are at the point of a nervous breakdown. They are afraid that this so-called honesty about our history has brought us to a loss of confidence about what's right in America. There is more liberty, there is more prosperity, there is more given to charity in this land than any nation in the history of the world. The progress out of poverty of the black and the rural poor of our land in the last decade has been the greatest social movement away from poverty in the history of the world. Yet we're still teaching our young people that we're so rotten we ought to burn the whole place down.

This is the problem of loveless criticism. I am tired of the Church of Jesus Christ taking it on the chin at every turn. I will not sit still with people who hate the name of Christ, who have no use for Him, who will not make sacrifices, but who think they have the right to criticize the Church.

If we foster a critical spirit, we soon discover that we are not honest, loving critics, but hostile, alienated, angry, hate-filled people who project the poison of our life on everyone we meet. Jesus Christ did not come to tear people down; and we do not serve the cause of Christ nor stand in His tradition if we feel that God has called us to do what Jesus did not do.

One of the things we learn about people who are chronically negative, hostile and critical, whether in a marriage or family or a society or a church, is that they reveal more about themselves than about those they criticize. Freud pointed out that most of this is projection—what we hate in others is true about ourselves. We soon reveal by our critical spirit that the trouble is not outside us. The trouble is in us.

If criticism is necessary, and we want to avoid being destructive and loveless, how can we as Christians be true counselors? First, before you open your mouth, purify your motives in prayer. (I have never had to apologize for something I didn't say!) When I have done this, God has helped me and purged me of resentment or jealousy or any other wrong motivations.

Second, we have to earn the right to criticize. It's only when we have demonstrated adequately our basic love so the person can feel it, that our criticism becomes tolerable.

One of the best things that happened to me as a young cleric who was pushing to change things in my denomination was the fact that they withheld my ordination for a few years due to a technicality. I had a ministerial license, which meant I wasn't quite as free to say what I wanted to at the Annual Meeting. It was good for me to have to keep my mouth shut for five years. By that time I had demonstrated that I was serving my denomination well and contributing to it's growth. God had blessed the little church that had come into being under our ministry, and it was a loyal church and a contributing church. Then I had earned the right to say something, because at this point my love for the church was demonstrated and people were more ready to hear what I had to say.

It's the same with children. You can give only ten percent of criticism; you must give ninety percent love and approval. If you change the proportions, the child will read rejection in what you say. We should have ninety percent love and ten percent disapproval all the way along the line. We ought to weigh how we come across.

Sometimes God speaks to me about criticizing others. "What has been the relationship? What you say may be true, but have you spent enough time developing love and confidence so that the person will receive what you have to say?" I'm not called to speak for the love of speaking. I think when God asks me to criticize it's because He wants something good to come from it. We must earn the right to criticize.

Third, let us realize that there are different ways of saying things. A psychologist once demonstrated a couple of ways of expressing unhappiness about a situation without making the other person feel like a skunk. Instead of saying, "You no-good so-and-so, you make me so mad!!! I can't stand you!" just say, "I feel very tense and angry right now." You're expressing your own feelings, rather than describing the other person's failings. It gives the person the opportunity to respond. It involves Christian humility—not judging the other person, but confessing how *you* feel. "I'm having a reaction right now. I feel very angry right now. I feel very indignant." The other person gets the point, but there's a little room to talk. And he can say, "Well, I'm sorry I've caused this reaction in you."

Finally, avoid public humiliation, whether it's to your children, your spouse, your fellow Christian. Our Lord Himself established the order for church discipline: "If a brother sins against you, go to him privately and confront him with his fault. If he listens and confesses it, you have won back a brother. But if not, then take one or two others with you and go back to him again, proving everything you say by these witnesses. If he still refuses to listen, then take your case to the church. . . ." (Matt. 18:15–17, *TLB*). Experience has taught me that when I haven't followed that procedure it has been disastrous; when I have followed it, it has been redemptive. Avoid the public dressing-down until the last moment, and then let it be only as an official act of the church.

To exist is to be criticized. To act is to be doubly criticized. To take a step of commitment and faith is to risk drowning in criticism. That is more inevitable even than taxes because there are no loopholes. Not even Jesus, the sinless One, was excluded.

Since criticism will come, we need to learn how to handle it. The first step is to learn to be honest with ourselves. Part of our sensitivity is the fear that the criticism may be true. I have seldom been shaken up by criticism which was preposterous. The only time I really get upset is when it's the truth, or I'm afraid there might be a germ of truth in it. If we love virtue and want to be right, criticism will never be easy to take, because it would make us admit a fault. But if we have practiced honesty about our own failings and have given up trying to convince everyone that we are perfect Christians, the truth about us isn't going to be quite so damaging. We'll be able to take it. When they come and say, "You so-and-so, you know what you are and you know what you do?" I'll be able to say, "Is that all? I can tell you a few more things!"

We can practice a basic inner resting, not in our own righteousness, but in the righteousness which comes through Jesus Christ. This gives the greatest stability in the face of adverse criticism that any of us can have. The extent to which criticism sends us into a spiral is the extent to which our peace of mind rests, not on the righteousness of Christ, but on the righteousness which we have manufactured in the interests of a favorable public image.

Secondly, study the face of your critic as you listen to his words. Sometimes you will discern the face of a person who is very troubled, very angry, very sick. Don't let this keep you from receiving what truth there might be in his words—God sometimes speaks through sick people. You're really mature when you can profit from even unkind and unloving criticism. I am not there yet, myself, but that's where I want to go.

Remember, too, that much criticism is based on ignorance. Many people who criticize merely betray their ignorance; and ignorance is to be pitied, not despised.

Third, find loving relationships with people who can give you moral support. Get close enough to them so that they know your faults and you do not need to conceal them. Entrust yourself to these people; they are the ones whom God will send to bear you up in the times of harsh and angry criticism. The opinion of those who know you best is most decisive.

The trouble with many of us is that we are so afraid of criticism that we withdraw from an open and loving relationship with people. It is this isolation caused by our fear of being criticized that makes us most vulnerable to criticism, because there is no one close enough to us to hold us up and to sustain us during that time.

Fourth, accept even unkind criticism graciously, but do not cower. I realize this is a hard one to understand.

There may be truth in the most unkind and cutting remarks. There are, however, some people who feel the fastest way to avoid criticism is to cave in and say, "Oh, my, you're right," when in fact it may not be right. Don't cower if your critic is wrong.

I have a dear friend who is a minister. He has the personality trait of feeling that any criticism that anybody has for him must be right. He had some neurotic, overweening, hostile members who just loved to come into the office and tell him what was wrong with him. I said, "Dick, nobody does that to me."

And he said, "I know why they don't—just one 'I beg your pardon' with your booming voice and that would settle it." (My errors and problems are in the other direction!)

We must be gracious. But God has not called upon us to plead guilty in the face of our innocence. God did not say that humility meant playing the role of a pincushion. There is a limit in which Christian decency must say, "That is enough!"

Finally, remember that time vindicates the godly. When you're under the heat, that's a hard thing to remember. I remember the time that a husband told me that his wife was having an affair with another man. This was subsequently verified by a witness. As the relationship continued I faced one of those most unpleasant moments that become a pastor's duty: I had to talk to the wife. I went up to the house, rang the doorbell, was invited in, and I began to say, "I have talked with your husband and he has told me"—when I was blasted with hysterical screaming about "that hypocritical church . . . those self-righteous people . . . and you're the worst one of them all. . . ."

These tirades don't shake me up anymore. In fact, I'm going to have a recording made to save people's breath. I'll tell them, "Before you get all worked up—here, play what you're about to say." It's a standard speech. I've heard it dozens of times. The standard response when the minister knocks, and there is chocolate all over your mouth, is to say, "What a bunch of unloving hypocrites you all are down there. If you're going to start on me why don't you throw all those proud hypocrites out of the church?"

The Lord gave me restraint with the woman because I had heard it so often. Finally I said, "Remember this: you will find that your dearest friends are not those who always compliment you for what you have done, but those who have had the courage to look you in the eye and say, 'You're wrong.'" With that I escaped with reasonable soundness of body from the house.

Then I had to wait. You don't ever want to be hasty in church discipline matters. The thing that made it hard to wait was that this was not an open secret. It was known only by the closest member of the family. Not even the Board of Deacons knew. And the woman immediately got on the telephone with her closest friends to tell them what an unkind, un-Christian, unloving man I was, and how unfit I was to be a Christian minister. Of course, sooner or later, the minister hears everything. But what could I do? I could say nothing. I had to be vilified without having a chance to reply. It was hard to look at people who were my dear friends and whom I shepherd, and have them turn away in disapproval. It was hard!

Then came the day she came back to church. She sent a letter which is one of my most treasured possessions: "Dear Pastor Larsen, I have severed the relationship. I am back with my husband. It was not easy for me to hear what you had to say, but I am at last convinced that you are indeed a man of God. Thank you for the courage to speak." (And by the way, I never had to go around and straighten out the rumors she had spread. The Lord let her unplug all the damage.)

In the final analysis the Lord is our vindicator. The most desperate trouble we can get into is to decide that we make our own name right. A person very close to my family was unjustly slandered and could not wait for God to vindicate her. She died unemployable and starving because she could not learn to trust God to vindicate her.

Gracious God, teach us how necessary criticism is. Help us to see, however, that much criticism is not loving and help us to be loving when we must criticize. As unkind criticism is inevitably our lot and one of Satan's cheapest implements, teach us how to handle it and to leave the vindication to You. Amen.

The Lord despises those who say
that bad is good, and good is bad.
It is senseless to pay tuition to
educate a rebel who has no heart
for truth.   Proverbs 17:15,16, *TLB*

17

A
HEART
FOR
TRUTH

It is possible to be educated and to have no heart for truth, for truth has a moral dimension which education cannot provide. If the moral dimension is coupled with education, education becomes an invaluable asset. Otherwise education merely creates a generation of clever devils.

There was an interesting article in the *Wall Street Journal* by Edwin McDowell on Professor Sidney Hook, who recently retired from his position teaching philosophy in New York. Hook is regarded by some as "the one significant political philosopher that our country has produced this century."[1]

Now Sidney Hook is no fundamentalist. He is no conservative Republican. He stands in the very liberal tradition of our land. He has been profoundly influenced in his thinking by the social upheavals and violence that have occurred in American colleges and university campuses. Hook has said that he wants to be remembered as "an exponent of the democratic way of life—for teaching that democracy and freedom can live in fruitful union."[2]

When asked if he has any regrets after so many battles over so many years, Hook hesitated, then replied, "Like John Dewey, I've always regarded intelligence as the central value in the moral economy. Intelligence indicates how to reconcile such conflicting values as love, kindness, virtue, duty and honor. But now toward the close of my life, as a result of the upheavals on campus, I face the problem that Dewey and I never came to grips with—namely, that intelligence is necessary but it isn't sufficient for the good life. We need, in addition, moral courage to act on intelligence."[3] Education must have, in addition to learning, a commitment; or as the writer of the Proverbs says, "a heart for truth," not simply a head.

"The Lord despises those who say that bad is good, and good is bad." This is the crisis of our times. We may have more knowledge and learning and education on a mass scale than we have ever had; but it is nonetheless true that there is more moral confusion in our time than in almost any previous epoch. Men are confused about what is right and what is wrong. This is the central crisis. It is, if you please, the erosion of the moral life.

This has happened before, even in very religious times. If you look at the Middle Ages, you will see that the church itself had become corrupt. While it mouthed one truth it lived another. This induced such moral confusion that society could be held together only by the imposition of strict rules, depriving people of their freedom. Hence the founding of the Holy Office of the Inquisition, an attempt to protect the establishment of the time from the searchlight of truth. Truth became the enemy of the church, rather than its handmaiden. This has happened time and again in history.

Today we have a question about morality itself. This arises from the pluralism of our times. Atheism and Christianity, Mohammedanism and evangelicalism, every form of morality is in collision. This has given rise to two things. One is relativism which is not the recognition that people believe different things, but the ideology that since there are so many beliefs there is no right belief. Relativism gives way to individualism which says, "Well, it's all a matter of how you personally feel about it." This is not the same as tolerance—it's worlds apart. With relativism it is all too easy to jump to the conclusion that there is no right and wrong. Even the disapproval of murder and violence is removed and made relative. If you don't believe that, read Jerry Rubin's book entitled *Do It*. With only relativism, there is no right or wrong.

Then there is secularism which thinks of man, not as created in the image of God, but as an animal organism seeking to survive in his environment. Ethical judgments are no longer based on transcendental goals, that is with reference to the will of God, but in terms of how the individual animal may survive in the happiest possible condition. This gives rise to what the philosophers call "egoistic hedonism." If it's fun, do it; if it isn't, skip it! This attitude provides the justification for doing "enjoyable" things that formerly were not done because they were considered wrong. The criterion for behavior standards is no longer a matter of right and wrong, but what it *feels* like.

Antinomianism is another result of secularism. Noticeable even in the history of Christianity, antinomianism teaches that the moral laws of God are nothing. A certain off-branch of psychoanalysis goes beyond that to indicate that morality is the only evil thing in this world.

Modern social science teaches that anything which occurs in nature is natural. Any perversion or act is, therefore, naturally all right, as long as a person does not feel guilty about doing it. According to this viewpoint, if brutality and cruelty are a person's way of life, you don't condemn his behavior or say he is wrong; you just make sure you avoid him. This is the kind of thinking that God despises: "The Lord despises those who say that bad is good, and good is bad."

Paul, in his epistle to the Romans, says that abandoning God leads to the ultimate manifestation of human iniquity and depravity, and brings society to the brink of collapse. (See Romans 1.) Today we see it happening. We stand on the brink of social dissolution; all moral distinctions are sinking into the subjectivity of human opinion.

This whole trend of relativism has led to the decay of the educational process. Education must have a moral balance. Unless there is a heart for truth then even morality becomes a casualty.

I pointed out the tragedy of the medieval church

when it would not face the light of truth upon its own practice. The same thing happened in the fundamentalism of the 1920s and 1930s. I speak of it both sympathetically and critically, for there were probably none who clung to the historic Christian faith so strongly as these people. Because the educational system of that time had largely repudiated biblical Christianity and had adopted the rationalism of the German universities, virtually all the major theological seminaries in this country were teaching error.

The only people left to defend true Christianity were people without an education. The uneducated people had not been corrupted. The tragedy was that to protect themselves, fundamentalists lost their heart for inquiry and truth. In an error of strategy not of intent young people were told, "Now don't go to the university, and above all avoid the theological seminaries because they will corrupt your faith." They were not reacting to a bogeyman; these schools really were dangerous places because they were largely hostile to the Christian faith. In attempting to save themselves by pointing a suspicious finger at the educational process, the fundamentalists planted in the hearts and minds of a generation of young people the idea that truth was dangerous and inquiry was perilous.

Now you put that seed into the mind of a young person and you have created tomorrow's infidel; so that defense against unbiblical teaching became the greatest downfall of the faith. Don't ever try to convince a young person that truth is dangerous. You'll only convince him that he ought to embrace the other viewpoint. This has been a tragedy of our times.

Let no one assume that extreme fundamentalists are the only people who are afraid to look at and explore the truth. It is the problem that any group feels when it holds its convictions with great vigor and tenacity. The radical left of American politics has manifested this same fear of open discussion. Herbert Marcuse, the Marxist philosopher, would abolish freedom of speech in his new society. The American academic community, which has championed freedom of expression as the indispensable quality of the American university, has been showing a surprising desire to stifle the free expression of ideas. While it has demanded the right of revolutionaries and radicals of the left to freedom of speech, it has vigorously sought to deny the same freedom to those on the right.

An interesting example of this is to be found in the case of Professor Willian Shockley of Stanford University. A winner of the Nobel prize in physics, Dr. Shockley has advanced the thesis that the Negro is intellectually inferior to the Caucasian by virtue of his genetic makeup. Such a position certainly lies outside of the field of Dr. Shockley's expertise and is repugnant to the Christian understanding of man. Yet Professor Shockley's classes have been interrupted at Stanford University, and at Sacramento State University, the president denied him the right to express his views. Such an example is not untypical. Statesmen have been shouted down and universities closed in an attempt to block the free interchange of ideas. We can be thankful that the worst of these disruptions seems to be over.

The fact that Christianity has nothing to fear from

a free and open discussion of the truth is amply demonstrated in American history. The founding fathers created an open society without an established religion. They were not, by and large, men of genuine Christian faith. Christianity was at low ebb and rationalism or deism was the prevailing philosophy. Less than ten percent of the population belonged to churches. Contrary to popular opinion, this nation was not born through faith in the God of the Bible. Many people feared that the new freedom of religion and speech would spell the end of the Christian faith.

But what happened in this free and open environment? Could Christianity continue to exist in a nation which gave it no money and whose public universities ridiculed the Bible? In 1797 a revival began under George McGreedy Price. In 1801, 1820, 1840, and 1850 revivals swept across the country. In the latter half of the century, men such as Finney, Moody and others led the nation forward. Today more than half of the population is affiliated with churches. Despite some attrition in some of the liberal Protestant churches of our time, Christianity has never become so powerful in any nation as in America. And it did this without public money. An open society is the place where the Christian faith survives most vigorously.

We have flourished in the bold experiment of freedom. Thus to defend the freedom to pursue the truth is a most Christian task. To pursue the truth without regard to its consequences is not dangerous for a Christian. It is the only safe redoubt. In so doing we seek Christ, who Himself is the truth. In that truth we find our freedom.

A heart for truth is the only thing that makes any pursuit of knowledge valuable. It is the only basis on which a man can find a relationship to God. Let us, then, end our cynicism about truth on the one hand and our fear of truth on the other. Let us hear the wise man when he declares: "The Lord despises those who say that bad is good, and good is bad. It is senseless to pay tuition to educate a rebel who has no heart for truth." With that heart for truth we may seek the truth.

He who seeks the truth shall find Him who is the truth, even Jesus Christ. "If with all your heart ye truly seek me, then surely you will find me. Thus saith the Lord." Amen.

Lord, help us never to fear that truth is dangerous. Despite the scoffing of learned men, give us a heart for truth. Help us to perceive that beyond all human truth is He who is the Truth, even our Lord Jesus Christ. Amen.

1. Edwin McDowell, "Sidney Hook, Exponent of Democracy," *Wall Street Journal,* May 22, 1972.

2. McDowell, "Sidney Hook," *Wall Street Journal,* May 22, 1972.

3. McDowell, "Sidney Hook," *Wall Street Journal,* May 22, 1972.

Wine gives false courage; hard liquor leads to brawls; what fools men are to let it master them, making them reel drunkenly down the street!   Proverbs 20:1, *TLB*

ALCOHOL AND PIETY

Alcohol is a controversial subject, as are most social and ethical questions in our time. The Christian church has two basic views of alcohol: One is abstinence, and the other is temperance or moderation.

What does the Bible teach? Our text from Proverbs tells us that wine gives false courage; that hard liquor leads to brawls; and that men are fools to let it master them. It is difficult from that text to see where the Bible stands. Obviously the Bible is against drunkenness, but this passage does not tell us whether the Bible favors total abstinence or moderation.

There are two more passages on the use of alcohol in the book of Proverbs. Chapter 23 is really a classic: "Whose heart is filled with anguish and sorrow? Who is always fighting and quarreling? Who is the man with bloodshot eyes and many wounds? It is the one who spends long hours in the taverns, trying out new mixtures. Don't let the sparkle and the smooth taste of strong wine deceive you. For in the end it bites like a poisonous serpent; it stings like an adder. You will see hallucinations and have delirium tremens, and you will say foolish, silly things that would embarrass you no end when sober. You will stagger like a sailor tossed at sea, clinging to a swaying mast. And afterwards you will say, 'I didn't even know it when they beat me up. . . . Let's go and have another drink!' " (Prov. 23:29-31, *TLB*).

The next section is in Proverbs 31:

"And it is not for kings, O Lemuel, to drink wine and whiskey. For if they drink they may forget their duties and be unable to give justice to those who are oppressed. Hard liquor is for sick men at the brink of death, and wine for those in deep depression. Let them drink to forget their poverty and misery" (Prov. 31:4-7, *TLB*).

The writer of this passage recognized a couple of thousand years ago what medical authorities are saying now: alcohol is a mind-altering drug, but that doesn't make it entirely bad. There may be a legitimate use for it. It may be administered just as we administer morphine or other pain-killers. However, the more responsible a position one holds, the more careful one should be in the use of alcoholic beverages.

We find a dual tradition in the Old Testament. Persons who wanted to make the special dedication of the Nazarite vow, as recorded in Numbers 6, promised not to cut their hair, and not to drink wine or grape juice, not even to eat grapes or raisins or any other product of the vine, for the duration of the vow. This voluntary abstinence demonstrates that there have always been those in the Old Testament tradition who maintained abstinence from alcoholic beverages. But we must be honest with the data—the Old Testament nowhere imposes this standard on all people.

What about the New Testament? We see somewhat the same problem. People who believe very strongly in abstinence try to prove that the wine Jesus drank was only grape juice. But you cannot argue that way if you are really honest. There was no refrigeration. Plain grape juice would not keep; in time, it would naturally *become* wine.

Matthew records an incident that sheds some interesting light on the matter. John the Baptist was an abstainer, but it appears that Jesus was not. "For John the Baptist doesn't even drink wine and often goes without food, and you say, 'He's crazy.' And I, the Messiah, feast and drink, and you complain that I am 'a glutton and a drinking man . . .' " (Matt. 11:18,19, *TLB*). We have to recognize that in the New Testament, there are both traditions, moderation and abstinence.

Paul told Timothy that he should take a little wine for his stomach. (See 1 Tim. 5:23.) I think that Timothy was an abstainer. He did not feel that the use of alcoholic beverages should be a part of his practice as an elder in the church. So Paul had to say, "Now you are sick and you need this, so take it." It indicates again that we have some ambiguity in the Bible. There is a strong abstaining tradition in the Old

Testament and the New Testament, yet there is no categorical statement about it.

Then, you say, where have all the problems arisen over the question of abstinence? Why the temperance societies and the WCTU? Where did the Christian church get the emotional steam in the 1920s to get the Volstead Act passed which banned alcoholic beverages in our land?

To answer, we have to study the effects of alcoholism. We have to see the tragedies induced by alcohol. One place we have to look is alcohol's effect on certain cultures.

As cultures break up or go through transition, the danger of alcoholism rises. In a stable agrarian society there is a low rate of alcoholism. In cultures which are in collision and transition, the rate of alcoholism skyrockets.

Look what firewater did to the American Indians. The collision between the tribal culture and the advanced technology of the West caused the Indian culture to disintegrate. In the stress of this collision, alcoholism became almost endemic in the entire Indian population. Thus we had the stricture that alcohol could not be sold to Indians, because it was destroying them.

A similar effect was also noticed by the missionaries in Hawaii. The Puritan missionaries, who were sent out in the 1820s from New England, were given, in addition to their salaries, certain supplies. These included so many liters of whiskey in barrels. They could handle it; it was a part of the stable New England environment. When they got to Hawaii the whalers had beaten them to it, and alcoholism had broken out in the Hawaiian culture. By the 1840s or 1850s, the biggest battle the missionaries were fighting was the destruction of the entire population by alcoholism.

So they adopted a rule that Hawaiian Christians must abstain from alcohol. But the missionaries were still getting their little stash of whiskey from New England. Eventually they began to be concerned about the inconsistency. They were also under the impact of the big Methodist group—and the Methodists were the backbone of the temperance movement. By 1870 the liquor portion for missionaries was eliminated, and missionaries could no longer use alcoholic beverages.

At the time of the Industrial Revolution getting drunk was something that only the rich people could afford. But with the discovery of cheap distillation processes any working man could get drunk for a penny. And so in the cultural transition of the Industrial Revolution, alcoholism in both Europe and America went sky high. Family life began to disintegrate. Part of the religious awakening of that time was to fight "Demon Rum." The tradition of abstinence became dominant in America's Protestant heritage.

Christians were sure that if they were going to Christianize America they had to eliminate alcohol completely from the scene. The final triumph of the American Protestant empire was to pass the Volstead Act, thus introducing the era of Prohibition.

But Prohibition grew increasingly unpopular and unworkable. By 1932 it became a popular election issue to repeal that act. We have been wallowing in our booze ever since. We have really not become as Christian as we had assumed.

As I look at the present stance of the church, with its dual tradition of abstinence and moderation, I find that I must criticize both.

The abstaining position tends to raise total abstinence to a category of absolute truth. Those holding this view readily assume that to drink is to be drunk—and that is not true. This has tended to become a kind of legalism by which we judge other Christians. We must draw the line—but how can we draw a line that would have kept our Lord Jesus out of the church?

The temperance or moderation tradition, on the other hand, is naïve. These people assume that being a Christian somehow gives you a perfect moral ability so that alcohol does not become a problem. Many people who have been in a Christian family for two or three generations just have not experienced the ravages of alcohol that others have. They do not realize how serious a problem alcohol can be in a person's life.

These are times of unparalleled social change—they are as great in terms of social change as any of the cultural collisions that occurred in the past. Half the beds in Los Angeles General Hospital are occupied by people who are there because of drug abuse or alcoholism. This is one of the major problems of our country. Alcohol is a mind-altering drug.

According to the U.S. Public Health Service, there are an estimated 9½ million alcoholics in America. (An alcoholic is defined as someone for whom the use of alcoholic beverages has produced serious complications in his health, his family life or his vocational life.) Nine and one half million alcoholics out of 100 million people who drink (in a population of 200 million Americans)! That means that between nine and ten percent of those who drink in the United States are being destroyed by alcoholic beverages. You can see why liquor should be classified as a dangerous drug. The FDA would not license for unlimited use a drug that ran this kind of risk.

The National Safety Council reports that out of the more than 50,000 traffic deaths that occur in our country in a given year, 25,000 of those fatalities are drink-related accidents. Why is there so little public concern about this tragedy—this slaughter—which over the years is killing more than all our wars have ever killed or maimed?

Professor John Kaplan's book, *Marijuana: The New Prohibition,* points out a series of studies made by medical experts which indicate that between forty and eighty percent of all homicides are drink-related.[1] They occurred while the party was drinking. Alcohol is directly related to the crime rate.

We are living in the crisis of the drug culture; we are all shaken by seeing young people destroyed. But the fact is that drug abuse among young people is nowhere near the serious national health problem that alcoholism is. I'm not saying that pot is better than booze—but booze is used a whole lot more than pot.

One of the strongest arguments used among young people against the use of marijuana is that it leads to hard drugs. But an interesting study reported in *The Medical World News* for December 3, 1971 indicates that alcohol, not marijuana, is the drug used by a high percentage of people who later become heroin addicts. The abuse of this substance is considered one of the chief causes of failure in Methadone maintenance.

In a series of studies researchers concluded that in about half of our heroin addicts, had intervention been made at an earlier age, the diagnosis would have been alcoholism or alcohol abuse instead of drug addiction. The phenomenon has implications for the prevention of heroin abuse. The essence of the study is that alcohol is more firmly established as a road to heroin addiction than is marijuana. We have been trying to tell our young people to stay off pot because they might become heroin addicts, but we ought to analyze the significance of our use of alcohol.

Professor Kaplan, in his book, says that marijuana and alcohol are dangerous drugs. "We let people over twenty-one use alcohol, so let's do the same for marijuana."[2] But that won't solve anything. You and I know that minors have no trouble getting booze if they really want it; likewise, they would have little trouble getting pot that was "for adults only."

What can we suggest as a Christian view of booze? I give you my answer, recognizing that there are two positions in the Bible and in the Christian church. In the light of the present stress I have determined that abstinence should be the road for me. Alcoholism does not just happen—it is related to the emotional structure of the personality. A person may drink "safely" for thirty years, and then encounter some sickness or job crisis and become an alcoholic. We have developed some new jargon to describe this:

the "dry alcoholic" is the person who will become an alcoholic sooner or later if he uses alcohol at all. Since I have two grandfathers who were alcoholics before they were converted, I have every reason to believe that I could become a real alcoholic very easily. I could well be a dry alcoholic. I don't want to take a chance on finding out!

My second reason for abstaining relates to my responsibility to my Christian brother. Paul discusses the fact that while we have liberty as Christians, there are areas in which we should voluntarily limit ourselves because of the possible effect on our brother. If through my example and encouragement a brother is led into alcoholism, then Christian love says I ought not to set that example. The chances of being a "dry alcoholic" are one in ten. I have two children, so there is a twenty percent chance that one of my children will be involved in a tragedy involving drink. As a pastor, I have hundreds of people in my flock. One in ten would mean that I would be willing to jeopardize scores of my sheep in the name of my Christian freedom. I don't want that responsibility. I feel like Billy Sunday, who said, "I will fight booze until Hell freezes over; and then I will buy a pair of skates and fight it on ice."

Having said that, I hasten to add that I am not now exegeting Holy Scripture. I do have a right to speak on this question even though the Holy Scripture does not speak specifically on it. Paul, you recall, cautioned people not to get married because of the stress at that time. Marriage is ordained of God, but Paul indicated that there may be times in the course of history when the social upheaval would cause some people to forego the privilege of family life. The Bible introduces the idea that there are times of crises when we have to restrict our activities in order to cope with the situation in which we live.

The church has done this before. You cannot find chapter and verse in the Bible that tells you that slavery is wrong; yet I do not think that the church was in error about God's will when, one hundred thirty years ago, it began to say that slavery was dehumanizing and ought to be abolished.

So I think today we have a right to speak on alcohol. I realize we can be faulted because in our traditional evangelical churches the only social issues we ever tackle are divorce, booze, prostitution, and abortion. We can be rightfully accused of having neglected questions of poverty, racism, and injustice. We must also address ourselves to those issues as well, so that we are not simply the special pleaders for Protestant taboos.

Finally, let us recall that the church cannot legislate for its members in the area of personal practice regarding alcohol. We cannot make this a part of church law. It would be going beyond the rights that the Scripture has given. Some Christians, because of their culture and tradition, do use wine and other alcoholic beverages in moderation. I sin against God and the church sins against God if we insist that these people are less than Christian because of it. If in their hearts before God, and considering the data available, they arrive at a different conclusion than mine, I am bound by law to accept their different standard. I cannot impose either a written sanction or a sanction of attitude against these brothers. I protest as strongly against the attitude of condemning your brother for a differing opinion, as I protest against booze in the first place.

The church is the custodian of the Word of God, and we seek to interpret the will of God for the issues of our conscience. But the church's fundamental task is not to enforce virtue upon people by acts of legislation or proscription. Sometimes we must teach law and ethics, but the essence of the church is proclamation of the grace of God. We do not fulfill our mission until we emphasize the grace of God more strongly than the Law of God.

One of the greatest tragedies of the church is that sometimes it has so inveighed against drunkenness that it has often not extended the hand of compassion and mercy to the person who is lost and trapped in his iniquity. The same can be said about drugs or sex abuse or anything else. The strident tone of the church's wrath has muted the voice of compassion, so that many who have found themselves in trouble have said, "The church is the last place I want to go. I don't need to be whipped anymore—my sin has whipped me. I need the words of God that say there is forgiveness in Jesus Christ and there is grace to overcome my problem." I want to be remembered not as the man who came and pointed the finger at someone and said, "You're doing wrong!" but as the man who said, "I realize how helpless you are. I have a friend, Jesus Christ. He can forgive you and make you whole."

Father, help us to be governed by Holy Scripture, to be careful that in our emotions, as well as in our words, we shall not go beyond Scripture in judging our neighbor. Help us to respect the right of our fellow Christian to make his own decisions. But lead us also into a Christian approach to the tragic social and personal crises that this problem has produced. May it affect us as we make decisions with regard to our personal conduct. May it heighten our dedication to being ministers of reconciliation, that we may weep over the erring ones, lift up one fallen, and tell them of Jesus the mighty to save. In His name. Amen.

footnotes

1. John Kaplan, *Marijuana: The New Prohibition* (New York: Simon and Schuster, Inc., 1971), pp. 276–282.

2. Kaplan, *Marijuana*, pp. 357,358.

Keep away from angry, short-tempered men, lest you learn to be like them and endanger your soul.

Proverbs 22:24,25, *TLB*

THE
HORROR
OF
HATRED

Hostility is a good deal like poison oak. It belongs to the plant life of the emotions. Flowers and plants and shrubs in the emotional life can be nourishing and pleasing, but they can also be very deadly things that infect and destroy. Part of wisdom in life is to know the difference when you go for a walk in your emotional garden. You need to know which plants to cultivate and which to discourage. You particularly need to know how to handle the poison oak of the emotions, human hostility.

Hostility grows in clumps. It is seldom found in an isolated condition. It grows in groups of people. That's why the wise man advises, "Keep away from angry, short-tempered men, lest you learn to be like them and endanger your soul." If you find yourself in the group you will contract the disease.

Hostility is infectious. Sometimes it is even contagious. It is not derived solely from our inherited, genetic, emotional makeup. It is an attitude which we pick up from the environment around us. Hostility in the home, which is a social group, will be conveyed to the children at a very early age. A very angry, hostile father or mother will produce anger in children. When you encounter a child who has a great deal of hostility and rage, you can figure that this was probably contracted in the home.

Sometimes we forget that the most important things we teach our children are things we are not consciously teaching. Angry, hostile parents produce angry, hostile children. You say, "I'm a mean, hostile, angry person and it's due to my father who was a mean, angry and hostile person." And your father can blame his father, who in turn can blame his father. We can go right on back to Adam and Eve—which is excellent Christian theology, but a lame excuse.

We have a capacity to communicate hostility to people. We tend to get what we give; we tend to produce in others what we have in ourselves. Hostility tends to produce hostility, as love and kindness tend to produce love and kindness.

Even among churches, there are subgroups that become hostile. Some churches exist by quarreling. They almost need it. Hostility, anger, rage and conflict have become a way of life for them. Every issue, every problem, is accompanied by dissent and anger.

Other churches and groups are characterized by a spirit of love and gentleness. They seek to settle differences of opinion through loving conversation rather than through angry debate. Of course, you never find a pure type; that's elementary sociology. But we can develop generalizations about the differences between two groups. For example, take an encounter with a person who has a great tragedy in his life, such as alcoholism. In one congregation this individual is treated with rage and condemnation. Another congregation will respond with compassion and intercession in prayer.

Evil can invade the church so that hostility and rage become a way of life. This is one of the factors involved in church schisms. In any population or group a certain percentage of the people are angry and hostile. Angry, hostile people tend to make good reformers because they can split things down the middle, they can bring about a confrontation. And there are times when it is important to have a schism. As Protestants we are part of a schism. However, when you divide a group, the percentage of angry, hostile people in the section that leaves is much higher. It is very easy for these groups to become excessively hostile and angry. This was seen in many of the Reformation churches. Increase the percentage of angry, hostile people in a group, and if you're not careful the whole group can become predominantly angry, argumentative and hostile.

The church at Corinth was characterized by quarreling, bickering, and disputing. Paul had to keep writing them letters trying to calm them down. There was a tremendous divisiveness: "I am of Paul . . . I am of Apollos." Almost everything that was done became an issue for contention. Hostility had become the prevailing theme.

Hostility can pervade cultures and nations, too. One of the big problems in America is that with our large population, with all kinds of people who have all kinds of viewpoints, we have tended in recent years to become more violent, more hostile, more prone to conflict. In one sense this isn't new. There has been a lot of conflict and violence throughout America's history. I can't agree, though, with Rap Brown that violence is as American as apple pie. It's about American as poison oak! Violence has been a part of our history, but it has been a very bad part of our history.

The entertainment media have helped move us in the direction of violence. *Time* magazine has coined a new word, "carnography," to describe our current glorification of violence. An outstanding example is the audience reaction to the film, *The Godfather*. Audiences actually cheered the scenes of violence and brutality; in fact, the more gruesome and brutal the scene, the more the shrieks of delight. That illustrates the ominous situation we are in. Such a film appeals to that perverse love of cruelty which lurks in every human breast. Now it is socially acceptable to enjoy that cruelty rather than to control it.

I'm one of those people who think there are some things we ought to suppress. Cruelty, in one sense, is as human as love. But I don't want to cultivate my capacity to enjoy cruelty. We should struggle against cruelty, not glorify it in our recreational pursuits.

This problem of cruelty isn't new, of course. One of the great leaders of the church in the fourth century, Augustine, became concerned about the cruelty found in the recreation of the times. The Christian community was raising serious questions about gladiatorial fights, for instance, where a bloodthirsty audience shrieked and howled as one man killed another in a game. Augustine was instrumental, with other leaders of the Christian church, in influencing the Roman government to ban gladiatorial combat.

There were those of that time who said, "We ought to permit this because this allows the natural cruelty of people to be siphoned off in a more innocent direction. It keeps them from killing each other." We have people today who hold to this theory. "Pornography and carnography are really good for us," they say, "because we drain off the emotions and then we won't act it out in real life."

But Augustine was firmly of the conviction, as are many of our social scientists, that vicarious violence does not reduce human cruelty but escalates it. Violence in the media creates fantasies, and fantasies are preludes to action. They're rehearsals for the real thing. You ultimately act as you dream. This is the connection in a tragedy such as Kent State. The university students were reenacting the revolutionary drama of people against the establishment when they threw stones at soldiers trained to kill. To some extent that confrontation came out of the fantasy life. And when some of the students fell dead under the bullets of the soldiers, we had a shock wave in our culture. You never feel the bullets on television or in a novel. Augustine said the trouble with fantasy is that it allows us to participate without ever being impelled to action or enduring the consequences. Because of the way the fantasy life operates, young people can talk flippantly about revolution, drugs, violence and sex; they can create ethical standards which are totally divorced from their inevitable consequences and tragedy.

The Christian community ought to be aware of the seriousness of the systematic cultivation of cruelty and hatred that is taking place within our culture. We have, in the gospel of Christ, the antidote to this poison.

A second point about hostility is that it masquerades very well. "A man with hate in his heart may sound pleasant enough, but don't believe him; for he is cursing you in his heart. Though he pretends to be so kind, his hatred will finally come to light for all to see. . . . Flattery is a form of hatred and wounds cruelly" (Prov. 26:24–26,28, *TLB*).

One of the first things we all learned to do with our hostility, because it got us into trouble, was to pretend that it wasn't there. Only occasionally does hostility emerge in all of its cruelty. Usually it masquerades as something else. The more hostile and angry a person is, the more he develops the skills of disguise. This becomes a problem when it makes us wonder how to interpret people's motives when they are nice to us.

There are a couple of symptoms that can guide us in learning whether a lot of hostility is found in a personality. Most analysts of human behavior say that rigidity of personality, woodenness, inability to bend and make changes, are symptoms of suppressed rage. The person who can never change a schedule, the person who can never compromise a viewpoint or a method, is an angry person. Rigidity is a symptom which shows that a person is working very hard to control his rage; he's afraid it will break open on him. When Jesus attacked Pharisaism, He was saying, "This rigidity is covering up an awful lot of hate; it's laced up with all these tight rules that can never be bent."

Another symptom of hostility is "opinionation." As one of the most opinionated men I know, I speak from authority: we betray the hostility within us by our vehemence over little things. I'm not talking about the great issues of life, because we need to take a stand for truth. I don't think we should confuse low adrenalin and a lack of conviction with Christian virtue. But some of these little tiny questions can be argued with the same vehemence as the great issues. Some people can't seem to see things in their proper proportions.

Another symptom of hostility is criticizing others. One of the interesting things that a pastor notices is how his predecessor is regarded. Once or twice in a church, people went out of their way to tell me how much more they appreciated me than my predecessor. They thought that they were flattering me; but my wife used to say, "I wonder how soon it will be us!" The tendency to praise you to your face and to make favorable comparisons against other people may not be so much an evidence of their friendship and regard for you, but their way of managing hostility. You wonder when you'll become the bad guy who gets compared with the next one.

"Flattery is a form of hatred and wounds cruelly" (Prov. 26:28, *TLB*). I'm not arguing against saying nice things to each other and being kind and gracious.

We all need this sort of affirmation. But it must always be sincere and loving, never a form of manipulation.

Some people are kind and nice because they want to use you. Their flatteries mask real hatred. This demeans human language because the flatterer renders all kind words suspect. When I look a person in the eye and say, "I love you and I think you did a wonderful job," they wonder, "Is that an official thing pastors say in order to keep their public relations straight, or did he really mean it?" Thus the flatterer sins against the whole community, because he makes it difficult for us to receive kind and gracious words. He poisons the atmosphere for open expression.

The great historic example of the cruelty of flattery is Judas betraying Christ with a kiss. The kiss is the signal to the high priest's guard that this is the man who must be arrested. That may be why something as expressive of human affection and acceptance as a kiss makes many of us very uneasy; except when it comes from someone we really trust, we can't decide what it means. We have been betrayed too often by flatterers.

Hostility not only masquerades well and grows in clumps, but is easily confused with another plant which is essential to life—the plant of love. Notice Proverbs 27:5,6: "Open rebuke is better than hidden love! Wounds from a friend are better than kisses from an enemy!" (*TLB*). We can become confused by kind words which mask hostility and hatred; but there are sometimes frank and even cutting words which are motivated by love. It's very easy for us to hide from the truth by assuming that all criticism arises from hostility and never from love. The Bible teaches us

220

"faithful are the wounds of a friend." Love, if it is really love, has to be tough.

Our problem is that when the word of truth comes to us we're not ready to hear it. And it often comes to us as a word of criticism that's hard for us to accept. The person who gives us the criticism may be tense, and we interpret that tension as hostility. But love has to be tough.

A young woman came to me once and said, "One of my dearest friends from college was a fine Christian girl; but now I find that she is living with a man to whom she is not married. She has asked me to come over for dinner. I'm afraid to say anything to her about her relationships with this man, for fear that she will interpret it as judgment and hostility."

Isn't this how we all feel? We all run into situations like this, perhaps not as serious, but situations where something is wrong. And our society says, "Don't say anything." That's not love—in fact, that kind of silence is the flattery of hatred which says, "I want you and need you as a friend; I will not risk your disapproval by saying what I feel. I will act as if you were doing nothing." That's hatred—that's hostility. That's flattery. The only loving thing to say is "How come? How dare?" Faithful are the wounds of a friend.

Remember, however, you have to earn the right to wound a friend. Only when he is assured of your love for him as a person is it really safe. I'm always wary of these souls that go forth to wound everybody out of love. I wonder if it's really love that makes them the "Grand Protectors" of everyone else's virtue.

"Well," you say, "when a person tells me what I'm doing is wrong, is he expressing hatred toward me or is he expressing love?" You may never really know. Maybe it's a little of both. And maybe it isn't our business to interpret the person's motives. Maybe we should just ask ourselves if what they said was true.

When someone comes in with a criticism, I notice how he responds to my response. Hopefully I will say, "There may be something to that. I have a problem. I'm going to have to evaluate that." If I sense a feeling of relief coming over him, then I'm inclined to feel that he spoke from love and concern for me. But if he merely hits harder—then I think that it wasn't so much a concern as a need to cut and to hurt.

In greater or lesser measure we *all* suffer from hostility. Even depression is a form of inverted rage. It says, "I'm one of these nice people who goes off in a corner—I'm one of the loving types. I get depressed instead of getting mad." That's not true. You have self-directed hostility, which is not materially different.

I believe the real problem in the self is that we need to discover the Christian community. We cannot identify hostility and hatred in our own experience until we see it through the eyes of others. Unless we develop that kind of relationship, we're going to live a life of personal blindness. There is, in a sense, no solitary Christian. We all need the church, the community which strengthens and enlightens. We need to develop these relationships of trust so that we can express love and so that we can be honest with one another in love.

Two great men of antiquity wrote extensively. One

was the great stoic emperor, Marcus Aurelius, and the other was Augustine. Augustine wrote honestly about his sins—his autobiography is his confession. And he found forgiveness and grace in the Christian community. Marcus Aurelius, although he was an emperor and a great Stoic philosopher, never implied that anything he ever did or said was wrong. Augustine, not Marcus Aurelius, stands as the first modern man, according to psychologist William James.[1] We become great, we become strong when we become transparent and honest, not when we try to pretend that we have arrived. This is repentance and Christian community—to become honest through the eyes of our brothers and to become open to the transforming, renewing grace of our Lord Jesus Christ.

How like a poisonous weed, our Father, is hostility. It grows in relationships, in clumps. It masquerades as something sweet and kind when it is in fact cruel and deadly. We confuse ourselves too easily when Christian love and candor must speak to us a word of truth. God give each of us close friendships within the Christian community—friendships which are both loving and honest, so that before You we may see the truth and find renewal and change and growth in Jesus Christ. In His Name. Amen.

footnote

1. William James, *Varieties of Religious Experience* (New York: Random House Modern Library, 1902), pp. 42,44,108,353,464,486.

CONCLUSION

Both the length of a book and the extent of a series of sermons require an arbitrary end of the examination of Proverbs. The wisdom is infinite and neither time nor skill can expound it thoroughly. We have rather chosen the main themes of the book for our exposition. The first nine chapters of the Proverbs received relatively more attention because they thoroughly discuss the nature of wisdom. The rest of the book is written with reference to its main themes and current relevance. Should the omission of some of Proverbs cause the reader disappointment, then we have served him well. The only real way to grasp the ancient book is to stimulate the reader in his own lifelong pursuit of its wisdom.

There is, however, a larger question that can be raised. It is most difficult for "modern man" to believe that he can gain any new wisdom from ancient proverbs. The rise of our technology and the expansion of knowledge seemingly makes all previous learning obsolete. Certain people feel that there is little to be found in the "culture-bound, obsolete, musings" of ancient sages. For them, the Bible comes out of an ancient civilization with thought-structures so different from our own that there is really little they can contribute to us of worth. "Time makes ancient good uncouth." To these people the concept of a divinely inspired book being authoritative for our time is an absurdity.

Dr. Elton Trueblood calls this prevalent viewpoint the "disease of contemporaneity." His words speak for themselves:

"Contemporaneity, when it is a disease, is a very damaging disease, because it destroys the continuity of culture. . . . Associated with it is a really terrible conceit. I actually hear people say, 'What could Abraham say to us? After all, he never went faster than a few miles per hour. And any of us can go 600 miles an hour if we want to now.' 'What can Socrates say to us? He never saw a university with 30,000 students. He never really saw a big city. He didn't see any advanced technology. Therefore obviously his answers are not answers that are relevant to our day.' This, if it applies anywhere, is bound to apply all across the board. And what I want to say to these men is this: they have not really considered carefully enough the nature of the human problem. I want to say to them that a man can hate his wife at 600 miles an hour just as much as at six miles an hour, and that temptations to compromise with integrity are not really changed at all. Men have always had them; men will always have them. They are part of the predicament that man is man. And the notion that we are living in such a fresh time that wisdom has 'come with us' whereas nobody ever had it before—this I find to be an absolutely intolerable conceit."[1]

If the only way we can discern truth for our time is by what intellectuals happen to be thinking at the moment, by what criteria shall we judge whether they think rightly? Only the changeless can measure the changing. In the words of Paul Rees, "Only the durable is adaptable."

As a matter of fact, modern knowledge and technology have left us bankrupt with "truth for living." It would take the wisdom of Solomon to digest and apply all of the relevant psychological and sociological data to make the significant decisions of everyday life. Computer dating services have hardly introduced a revolution in romance and marriage. Indeed, the divorce rate has gone up since they began. Nor has it dropped with all the marriage counselors and psychologists who have been trained to help, valuable as they may be. No, modern empirical science has not given us a new wisdom for life.

The young of our time have revolted against the pompous pretentions of the new sciences. The rise of the counterculture among the young people is a direct challenge to the worship of science and technology. An acquaintance of mine is a well-known scholar and dean of one of our outstanding private colleges. His son was an exceptionally fine student who got top honors in his freshman year at Harvard. While home for a vacation, the dean noticed his son playing a strange game of cards. His son told him, "These are Tarot cards. They give me the secret wisdom by which I can make all my important decisions." Myriads of the younger generations have turned to the incantations of the occult because the wisdom of the world has proven so utterly foolish. When modern man cuts himself off from the Word of God in favor of his own wisdom, he ends up in witchcraft. When men forsake the biblical commandments, they end up like Saul of old on the road to Endor. There the coinage of witches and warlocks buy truth-for-living.

Certain modern theologians have attempted to salvage some wisdom for life without calling us back to the Word of God. They consider themselves Christians and seek to define everything in terms of love. Love is one element in the biblical religion not challenged in our time. Thus they have contrived to erect a scaffold of ethics that so emphasizes love as the standard of right and wrong that the force of the other biblical commandments is abridged. This is the viewpoint known as "situation ethics" which we have considered in our chapter on "Wisdom and Chastity." It is a sincere attempt to salvage a biblical emphasis without a full return to biblical authority. It has produced a rather rubber and flexible ethic that can do no more than plead, "Thou shalt not commit adultery ordinarily."

The failure of this viewpoint has been patent. All of us believe in morality and have the highest approval of love. It is only when obedience becomes costly that we look for an out. Love is an excellent alibi for breaking the law, particularly when we realize that it is a motive and motives are seldom pure. Our whole society has been shaken by the rationalizations for evil that this ideology has seemingly justified. Much of the Viet Nam conflict as well as anti-war violence itself, were justified under the name of situation ethics. Jeb Magruder, deputy director in the 1972 Republican presidential campaign who pleaded guilty to serious crimes, indicated that he had done so believing that breaking the law was justified by the "situation." Let us hope that Watergate will become the tombstone of "situation ethics."

The collapse of "scientific ethics" and "situation ethics" has led to a rebirth of concern in biblical ethics. The Jesus movement and the resurgence of conservative evangelical Protestantism indicate that the wisdom of which the Bible speaks is the only wisdom that can guide man whether he be ancient or modern. Such a renaissance is not simply a reaction formation or a return to absolutistic obscurantism. It is a return to a living tradition born of the spirit and guided by the written Word of God. It is seen not only in the rise of a competent biblical scholarship which reverences the Bible, but in a new vitality in the churches. It is seen in new art, music, and forms of worship. It is even seen in a return to the art of preaching, which the futurists had long ago consigned to the curiosa of obsolescence.

But let us ensure that the return to the Bible is in fact a return to biblical religion and not simply a new legalism. The relativism and lawlessness of our time creates a hunger for order and precision. It is easy in times like these to return, not to the wisdom of Proverbs, but to the legalism of the scribes and Pharisees.

Nor is the return to the Bible a return to extreme forms of ethical absolutism. David ate the forbidden showbread and Jesus healed on the Sabbath. All of the great ethical systems derived from the Bible throughout history have recognized the significance of extreme circumstances. They have neither been willing to modify the great commandments of the Bible nor to apply them in a ruthless and inappropriate fashion. The ethics of the Bible are neither absolutistic nor relativistic. They are better described as "objective ethics." That is, the commandments of God are to be interpreted always within the believing community and applied with the wisdom that the Holy Spirit grants. It is not our intention to articulate such a system in this book. Indeed such a system might tend initially to clarify and simplify biblical truth. But in the end it would lead people from the study of the Scriptures themselves. Inevitably it would both obscure and supplant the Word of God.

The days surrounding the coming of Christ were much like our own. The Jewish community was finding that its faith and life were being eroded by the blandishments of Greek and Roman culture. Young people were almost ashamed of their Jewish tradition. In order to save bliblical religion a number of movements sprang up to do battle against these unfortunate trends. Over a few generations there were a number of such groups. One of these groups became known as the "righteous ones." They later became known as the Sadducees, who by Jesus' time were anything but righteous. Another group who sincerely wanted to purify the Jewish nation were the "Separated Ones" otherwise known as the Pharisees. Yet so harsh and legalistic did they become, that they failed to recognize the Christ for whom they daily prayed. In fact, they crucified Him. The tragedy of these movements was abetted by the scribes who developed a body of scholarship and tradition aimed at keeping Judaism pure and giving a guide for living to everyday man. Ironically the greatest struggle Jesus had was not with the "compromisers," the "worldly" men of the day. Those whom He opposed, those who ultimately murdered Him were the "good people." Out of the legalistic tradition was ultimately to rise the Jewish Talmud, which was an attempt to clarify the Scriptures for thought and action.

These same trends have been evident in the history of the church. Legalism has always provided its new pharisees and scribes in each generation. Legalistic reasoning and ethics, as expounded through the high Middle Ages and up until very recently, "made the Word of God of no effect through tradition." What was started to simplify and clarify the Scripture ultimately supplanted it.

Now the sum of these historical references is this: In the return to biblical wisdom we must beware of the new legalism. I attended not long ago a seminar led by a devout and fine Christian leader. As with all of us who earn our living by writing or speaking, much was good, some was exceptionally good, and some was questionable biblical exegesis. We also received notebooks with hundreds of pages of interpretation and principles. These were by and large excellent. But the spirit that pervaded seemed scribal and legalistic. Again and again I thought: The New Talmud is being compiled. Somehow the Word of God is never quite sufficient. There is something in the human psyche that cannot quite live with Paul's *sola fide*—faith alone, or Luther's *sola scriptura*—scripture alone. What a man must have is faith plus deeds, Scripture plus interpretation. Alas, even a book of sermons such as this can contribute to this common and perennial error.

The Scriptures are not primarily a book of canon law or a codebook of ethics. They contain the divine commandments in the context of the life of the believing community. It is in the life of the believing community, in the study of the Holy Scriptures, that a person is filled with the Holy Spirit and discovers the wisdom of life. As such the book of Proverbs provides one of the most comprehensive statements of the divine wisdom anywhere in the sacred book. Its message is timeless. But it can never be used apart from Him toward whom the entire message points—Jesus Christ. Unless we move beyond the wise laws of the book to the Person of wisdom, our study will but lead to folly. In seeking wisdom, we seek Christ.

Such a message as this is not obsolete but contemporary. It is not that from which the young and the concerned have fled. It is that fountain to which they come. They have in fact come full circle. The rebellion of the young has now become a rebellion against the irreligion of our time. Sam Levenson puts it well concerning these young seekers:

"They have gurus but do not call them prophets. They will congregate for sit-ins, love-ins, talk-ins but do not call them congregations. They will not say 'amen' but they do say 'right on!' They have come not to the end but to the beginning of tradition. So many of our late pagans have become early Christians, and even earlier Jews. Welcome home."[2]

Such an invitation goes to everyone, not just the young, but to all those who earnestly seek wisdom.

"Yes, if you want better insight and discernment, and are searching for them as you would for lost money or hidden treasure, then wisdom will be given you, and knowledge of God himself; you will soon learn the importance of reverence for the Lord and of trusting him. For the Lord grants wisdom! His every word is a treasure of knowledge and understanding. He grants good sense to the godly—his saints. He is their shield, protecting them and guarding their pathway. He shows how to distinguish right from wrong, how to find the right decision every time" (Prov. 2:3-9, *TLB*).

Grant us, our Father, wisdom. We ask it in accordance with Your Word. We seek it, not to gain advantage over others, nor to fulfill selfish needs to advance our fortunes. We seek it that we may know Your will. We seek it more that we may know Him who is the Wisdom and Power of God—even Jesus Christ. For in seeking wisdom we seek Christ. So give us Him who shall not only point the way to life but shall lead us through the gates of life everlasting. Amen.

233

footnotes

1. Elton Trueblood, "Ideas That Shape the American Mind," *Christianity Today,* vol. XI, no. 7, Jan. 6, 1967, pp. 3,4.

2. Sam Levenson, *In One Era and Out the Other* (New York: Simon and Schuster, 1973), p. 321.

APPENDIX

Coordinated Reading Schedule

The chapters in this book follow the numerical sequence of the chapters in Proverbs. This reading schedule shows you how you can cover the many themes of Proverbs in units of related subjects. It is coordinated with the assignments given in the course designed for use with this book. Read the parallel assignments from the book of Proverbs and from this book *before* each class session.

ASSIGNMENTS	BOOK OF PROVERBS	WISE UP AND LIVE
	UNIT I WISING UP ABOUT GOD	
Session 1	Proverbs 1–3	Chapter 1 The Pursuit of Wisdom Chapter 2 Postures of Wisdom Chapter 3 Facets of Wisdom
Session 2	Proverbs 9	Chapter 8 Wisdom and Knowing God
Session 3	Proverbs 8	Chapter 7 Wisdom and Cleverness
Session 4	Proverbs 10	Chapter 9 The Wink of Woe
	UNIT II WISING UP ABOUT MYSELF	
Session 5	Proverbs 6,7	Chapter 5 Wisom and Deferred Pleasure Chapter 6 Wisdom and Filial Piety
Session 6	Proverbs 12	Chapter 12 Talk Is Never Cheap